The PEOPLE'S SENATOR

The Life and Times of David A. Croll

R. WARREN JAMES

Douglas & McIntyre
Vancouver/Toronto

In loving memory of Margaret L. James (1919-1983)

Douglas & McIntyre Ltd.
1615 Venables Street
Vancouver, British Columbia V5L 2H1

Canadian Cataloguing in Publication Data

James, R. Warren (Robert Warren), 1915–

  The people's senator

  Includes bibliographical references.
  ISBN 0-88894-671-6

  1. Croll, David A. (David Arnold), 1900– 2. Canada—
Politics and government—1935–* 3. Legislators—
Canada—Biography. 4. Canada. Parliament. Senate—
Biography. 5. Jews—Canada—Biography. I. Title.
FC631.C76J35 1990   971.064'092   C90-091556-0
F1034.3.C76J35 1990

Front cover photograph by Michael Bedford, Ottawa
Design by Arifin Graham
Typesetting by The Typeworks

Printed and bound in Canada
Printed on acid-free paper ∞

Contents

Preface

ONE OF MY TEACHERS ONCE TOLD ME THAT BIOGRAPHERS
ran the risk of either adoring or hating their subjects when
their task was completed. The goal of complete objectivity is
probably unattainable, but I have at least kept in the front of
my mind Adam Smith's remark about "the skill of that insidi-
ous and crafty animal, vulgarly called a statesman or politician, whose councils are directed by the momentary fluctua-
tions of affairs." David Croll has been a consummate politician all his adult life, endowing him with some special qualities and inhibitions. Apart from that, he has been a friend for
many years, and at the end of the hunt he remains a friend,
which speaks well for his forbearance. If Croll emerges un-
scathed from this biography, that result was not originally intended. I am neither by nature nor by training a hagiolater.

It should be understood that this biography was not commissioned. The project was my idea. However, I must offer
my heartfelt thanks to David Croll for giving me free access to
his papers, some of which are in the Public Archives of Canada, and for making himself available for a great many interviews. Nevertheless, Croll should be chastised with scorpions
for the unforgivable destruction of his personal papers before

he went overseas early in World War II. He had been involved in many controversial episodes during the 1930s and was reluctant to leave his personal papers in case he should be killed. Instead of sending them to the Ontario Archives or some other haven, he burned them and thus destroyed a piece of Ontario's political and social history that is hard to reconstruct.

John Munro was the editor of this volume, and I am greatly in his debt for his perspicuity in separating the wheat from the chaff and making the material much more readable. Apart from this important contribution, I have been helped in major and minor ways by archivists, librarians, relatives, friends and political and other associates of Croll. If I do not enumerate them individually, I hope they will be aware that I feel most grateful to them.

From its inception, this project has received very generous support from Samuel, William and Hyman Belzberg. I want to record my warm thanks to them for their continuing interest and gracious assistance.

Introduction

DURING THE HEYDAY OF THE CZARS, THE ASHKENAZIC Jews lived in large concentrations in eastern Europe. Because there were so many of them, they had a significant impact on the economy and their needs could not be ignored. Rigorous measures were taken to isolate Jewish communities, however, especially in Russia. There, the Jews lived mainly in villages or small towns, called *shtetls*, or *shtetlach*, within the Pale of Settlement, an area of twenty-five provinces established by Catherine II in 1791. About 4.8 million of the 5.2 million Jews in Russia at the turn of the century lived in the Pale of Settlement. The law confined Jews to the Pale, and to move outside the delineated areas required the permission of the police.

Conditions in the *shtetl* differed from those in the urban ghettos, where an oppressive and hostile majority enveloped the Jews. Jews predominated in the *shtetlach*, and often they were better off than the peasants, or muzhiks, in the surrounding villages. The economic activities of the Jewish communities varied widely, depending on the resources available and the skills of the people. Some communities were quite prosperous.

As a general rule, burdensome and discriminatory laws governed the types of jobs that Jews could hold and where they could go. In addition, Jews were prevented from mingling with ordinary Russian muzhiks; the risk that the peasants might be seduced by Judaism could not be tolerated. The resulting isolation fostered the traditional patterns of life among the Jewish people, who developed a conservative outlook on culture and religion and became bound up in the traditions of Judaism. Being isolated also allowed them to maintain their collective ideals. As a result, the impairment of civil rights of the Jews and the events in the outside world appeared to be either preordained or remote. Evolving Russian imperialism and the proceedings of the Duma concerned them less than the complexities of life in their own communities. As Nahum Goldmann observes about the inhabitant of the *shtetl*: "He was immersed in his own world, endowed with all the strength and dignity of a great past and a tradition dating back thousands of years. The only problems that had any meaning were the problems of Jewish life and these absorbed him totally."[1]

Although serious poverty and savage persecution occurred from time to time, literary and religious scholarship flourished. Many times throughout history, the economic and intellectual fortunes of an oppressed people have sunk in unison. The genius of the Jews in eastern Europe lay in the vitality of Judaism and the persistence of learning as a central fact of existence. Even the fantasies of Tevye the Dairyman about being rich involved founding a great academy of learning in Vilno.[2]

In discussing the traditional reverence for learning, Abba Eban quotes from the autobiography of Abraham Joseph Paperna (1840–1919), one of the early proponents of Jewish enlightenment (*Haskalah*):

All Jewish male children from the ages of four to thirteen were taught in *heder* [a Jewish school]. Although education was not compulsory for girls, they, too in most cases could read the prayers and the Pentateuch in Yiddish translation. A Jew of Kopyl [a small town in Russia] spared nothing for the education of his children. It was not rare for a poor man to sell his last candlestick or his only pillow to pay the *melamed* [teacher].[3]

Late in the nineteenth century, there was a spiritual and intellectual resurgence among the younger Jews in eastern Europe. The Messianic dreams of their elders had lost their appeal, and these young Jews rejected the passive attitudes that had often led to incidents of cruelty and despotism. An edict banning the attendance of Jews at high schools and universities after 1887 was a severe blow. Some young Jews could find refuge in the universities of Germany or elsewhere in western Europe, but this escape was open to very few. Many of the young people grasped at the promise of *Haskalah* and sought hungrily for a normal and free life.[4] Some abandoned their religion and cultural traditions and turned to revolution and violence, but most of them remained bound to the heritage of the *shtetl*. No influence was more potent than the codified rules that had been a beacon for centuries for Jews throughout the Diaspora.

One commentator, Max Dimont, has remarked about the Jews:

How did the Jews develop this flair for scholarship, this ability for theoretical thought, this passion for justice, this ability to peer into society and view it with such precision? The answer is that such scholarship was not an overnight growth but the very heart of the Judaic design for survival. Even in the ghetto, even when denied the educational facilities of the outside world, the Jews created their own educational institutions. The Talmud, although it did not answer the needs of modern living, was still the same Talmud of Grecian, Roman, and Islamic times, the Talmud of abstractions and legal logic that sharpened the mind. The Jewish passion for justice was part of an inherited tradition. Given a heritage that respected learning, that imparted justice, that taught its doctrines in abstractions, was it any wonder that the Jews should excel in the field of learning.[5]

Many of the spiritual leaders of the Jews had come from eastern Europe, where centres for Talmudic studies flourished. Apart from the biblical and Talmudic scholars, numerous pioneering writers and thinkers had come from this region. According to Herbert Feis, Jewish emigrants from Russia were the torchbearers of the Zionist movement.[6]

There is a risk of romanticizing life in the *shtetlach*. Whatever one may say about the cohesiveness and the social and cultural bonds within the *shtetl*, there were many reasons to want to leave it, including poverty, repression, a series of bad harvests, the possible conscription of Jewish young men, geographical confinement and the terrors of the pogroms, especially some of the intermittent but ferocious episodes of the 1880s. The brutal pogrom in Kishinev in 1903 must have convinced many Jews to listen more attentively to the tales of streets paved with gold across the Atlantic. By the end of the nineteenth century, the earlier waves of Jewish emigrants from Germany were replaced by a veritable flood of emigrants from eastern Europe. From 1880 to 1910, about one third of the Jewish population of that region emigrated. They spread all over the world, but the main destination was the United States. This was the *goldeneh medina* (golden country). Some, either deliberately or by accident, came to Canada.

David Croll's arrival in Canada was essentially an accident. He came, in Northrop Frye's striking phrase, "like a tiny Jonah entering an inconceivably large whale." He had very little baggage, but he unknowingly brought with him an enormous genetic and cultural inheritance.

ONE

Early Years

DAVID ARNOLD CROLL WAS BORN ON 12 MARCH 1900 IN A *shtetl* called Teterina within the Pale of Settlement, not far from Mogilev in Byelorussia (White Russia). Mogilev is about 320 kilometres east of Minsk. David's father, Hillel, was born about 1875, but there are no surviving records of his family history. David's mother was Minka Cherniak, who was born in 1880 and had lived in a neighbouring *shtetl*, Shiletz. David's parents had been married in the late 1890s, but the precise date is uncertain. David, who was named Dovid Avrum, was the oldest child. Two younger brothers were born in Russia—Leo, born in 1902, and Samuel, born in 1905.

Hillel was a salesman in the lumber trade. He mainly sold Russian lumber to Scotland, a trade that had been going on for many years. Like all the others in Teterina, the Crolls lived on a small holding; theirs was about four hectares. The fields lay between the house and outbuildings and the river, so there was a convenient pasture for their small dairy herd. There was a kitchen garden as well as field crops either for the farm animals or for sale. Both parents worked on the land and were able to maintain a decent standard of life.

In Teterina Jews were subject to civil disabilities, but there was no outright persecution or harassment. It is true that when the soldiers passed through the village, the young girls had to hide. Before David's mother was married, she used to take refuge in the house of the Russian Orthodox priest.

Croll's memory of life in Russia is sketchy. He recalls tying pieces of ice onto his boots and skating on the frozen Dnieper River in winter. He and his playmates also made primitive toboggans out of sacks and wooden slats to slide down the snowy hills. One day, he and the other children dug up what appeared to be a human skeleton. The authorities were summoned and it was later established that the bones were the remains of one of Napoleon's soldiers who had perished on that alien field.

The first member of the family to set out for the New World was Minka Croll's older brother Nathan, who emigrated shortly after the turn of the century. He had been a *melamed* in Russia, and after he landed on Ellis Island he learned from an advertisement in a Yiddish newspaper of an opening for a *shochet*, or ritual slaughterer, in Windsor. He started at this job but later turned to peddling in the countryside from a horse-drawn wagon. Then he opened a small grocery store and still later an apparel store. He finally established a chain of stores in Windsor, London and Hamilton dealing in men's and women's wear, furnishings and shoes. In a short time he progressed from a humble *melamed* to president of Cherniak and Company Limited. He typified the familiar story of the rise of the eastern European Jews in the commercial world.

While Nathan was still a young man, he persuaded his mother to come to Windsor and bring the rest of the family. She was a widow and had been left to bring up Nathan's other brothers: Jacob, Samuel, David, Meyer and Isadore. Nathan saved enough money to bring Samuel out first, and the two of them were able to bring out the rest of the family. Later Jacob, Samuel and David changed their name to Schwartz, the German equivalent of Cherniak, which comes from the word for black in Russian.

At roughly the same time that Nathan Cherniak embarked for the United States, Nathan Croll, Hillel's brother, a Talmudic scholar and Hebraist, had been induced to come to Detroit to teach in a *cheder*, or elementary Jewish school, that was being established there. In 1904, Hillel had been conscripted into the czarist army to fight in the Russo-Japanese War (8 February 1904 to 5 September 1905). Hillel Croll could have fled, as many young men did, but he felt a patriotic and religious duty to serve his country. By the end of the war, however, his future seemed so uncertain that he yielded to the urgings of his brother Nathan to come to the United States. Temporarily leaving his wife and young sons behind, he abandoned his homeland and set off for Detroit. By chance, his journey brought him to Windsor on a Friday night. Because he was a devout Jew and unable to travel on *Shabbes*, which was the following day, he went to stay with his in-laws, who had settled there some years before. The outcome was that he was to make his home on the Canadian side of the Detroit River.

Soon after his arrival, he was able to send for his family to join him. For David's mother, the normally wrenching experience of separation from friends, relatives and familiar surroundings was made easier by the fact that she could look forward to the welcoming arms of her mother and brothers in Canada.

Thus, in the spring of 1906, at a mere six years of age, David Croll sailed across the Atlantic, shepherded by his mother, who was to be his guiding spirit for many years, and accompanied by his two younger brothers, Leo and Samuel, and two cousins. Their group embarked from Libau, a Baltic port in Latvia now known as Liepaja, to Liverpool, whence after a three-week hiatus, they sailed on to Halifax. Croll's clearest recollections of the voyage were the numerous barrels of pickled herring scattered about the ship. Herring, black bread, potatoes and tea were the staple diet of steerage passengers, and the dreary weeks of ocean travel were a gloomy introduction to the Promised Land. However unpleasant life on board ship, at least David did not get seasick and was able to make himself useful fetching and carrying for his mother and other less hardy passengers. Minka Croll was well advanced in the pregnancy of her fourth child, so the trip must have sorely tried her in body and spirit.

After the voyagers landed in Halifax, they were loaded into colonist cars for the trip west to Ontario. These were equipped with wooden slatted seats that slid out to form a hard and uncomfortable bed. In addition, there was a hinged wooden shelf—a primitive upper berth. At the end of the car, there was a small, wood-burning stove, where the passengers could cook rudimentary meals, as well as a water barrel, a few cups and a wash basin. At intervals, the train would stop at stations where the passengers could obtain simple food such as cheese and eggs. These David Croll purchased for his mother by pointing, since none of them could speak English. It was a time of high excitement for the family, and the discomforts of their travel were balanced by the beautiful scenery and the happy prospect of reunion.

At the turn of the century, there were only fourteen Jewish families in Windsor,[1] which, according to the census of 1901, amounted to 149 individuals. By the time the Croll family arrived, this number was probably in excess of 200.[2] The presence of other Jewish families was important to Hillel Croll.

Hillel was by all accounts a kind and gentle man, imbued with a strong sense of justice stemming from his religious beliefs. A member of the orthodox Shaarey Zedek Synagogue, then located at Mercer and Brant streets, his great preoccupation was the study of the Talmud and the Torah. Indeed, his life could be said to have revolved around the synagogue and Judaism. He served the congregation in many capacities, one of them being to pass judgement on whether the meat offered the Jewish community conformed to the dietary laws. Although he did not have a full beard, he habitually wore a short stubble, which made him look older than his age. To be clean-shaven was not traditional among the orthodox. A cattle buyer for a local packing company, he travelled regularly through the southwestern Ontario counties of Kent and Essex, where he was known among the farmers for his unfailing honesty.

In Canada, the Croll family continued to expand. Maurice was born in 1906; Cecil, in 1908; and Evelyn, in 1911. Until they finished public school at age twelve or thirteen, David Croll and his brothers, like most Jewish boys the world over, also attended *cheder*, where they acquired a modicum of Hebrew, sufficient for ceremonial purposes if not for conversation. Yiddish, however, was the language of the home, since Jewish girls did not usually learn Hebrew.

Despite their differences in personality, Minka and Hillel Croll created a family that was very close. Hillel was no disciplinarian and never raised a hand to his children. Neither did Minka, but her promises of future retribution for present misdemeanours proved more effective than the rack. Always strong-willed, Minka, when still a young girl, had refused to marry the suitor selected by her parents because she did not like him, a shocking defiance of tradition. Shortly after her arrival in Windsor, Hillel declared that he wanted to return to Russia, where he could more easily carry out his religious duties; she replied that he could go if he pleased, but she was staying in Canada with the children.

The work ethic was strong among the Crolls, and any display of entrepreneurial talent was encouraged. At an early age, David began shining shoes to earn extra money, an activ-

ity that flourished during conventions. He also sold the Detroit *Free Press*, *Times* and *News* at the ferry terminal between
five o'clock and eight o'clock in the mornings and delivered
the *Windsor Record* after school each day. In later years, he
and his brothers were the sole source of the *Daily Racing Form*,
which they peddled at the three racetracks in Windsor, a
highly lucrative endeavour, since they could often sell several
hundred copies a day.[3] And when he was just fifteen, David
obtained the concession to sell sandwiches and soft drinks on
the special trains the Michigan Central Railroad ran from Detroit to Windsor during the racing season. Over two or three
summers, Minka sat up half the night making hundreds of
sandwiches for her sons to sell the next day. In addition, David and his friend Jacob Geller became owners of a newspaper
and magazine stand at the corner of Ouellette Avenue and
Sandwich Street.[4]

The principal supplement to the family income, however,
was the grocery store Minka opened on Windsor Avenue in
1914. The Crolls bought the building and moved their living
quarters upstairs. The boys helped with the deliveries and
made themselves generally useful around the store, when they
were not shining shoes or selling newspapers, racing forms and
sandwiches. Although by no means affluent, the family was
comfortable financially, and there was always enough money
to support community endeavours and required charities.

To Jewish parents, particularly those from eastern Europe,
the accomplishments of their children, especially the boys,
were a source of great personal satisfaction. Certainly the
Crolls impressed upon their youngsters the importance of attending to their studies. When Leo Croll was about thirteen,
he announced that he was quitting high school. Such hereti-
cal talk was not well received, and his mother said that if he
left, he would have to start looking for a job the next day. His
error revealed to him, Leo dutifully returned to his books. It is

also true, however, that no parental sacrifice to further the children's success was too great. When Minka Croll was a mature woman, there was a long period when she went out alone every Wednesday night. Hillel and the children assumed she was playing cards or otherwise socializing. Only years later did they learn that she had been attending night school to learn how to write better English so that she would be able to correspond with the boys when they were away at university. According to David Croll, his mother's strength of character made their family what it was.

When David Croll first entered public school, his English was at best halting. Fortunately, his classmates were a varied ethnic mix, and he was not singled out or discriminated against because of his foreign origin or his religion. After he moved on to the Windsor Collegiate Institute, later renamed the Patterson Collegiate and now defunct, he came under the influence of several outstanding teachers, among them Frederick Pierce Gavin and William Duff Lowe. But the greatest influence of all was Mary E. O'Donoghue, who taught history and literature. She saw much promise in Croll and determined that he would excel in her subjects. He did. It was the study of history that stimulated his interest in politics, a subject that has absorbed and fascinated him ever since.

In 1917, in an irresponsible moment, Croll and Jacob Geller lied about their ages and joined The Essex Scottish Regiment, hoping for overseas service. When Hillel Croll heard what his son had done, he paid a call on Lt. Col. E. S. Wigle, K.C., the commanding officer, who also was his lawyer. Once David's true age became known, his military career was quickly terminated.

David distinguished himself at the Windsor Collegiate Institute as a member of the football team. He had an outstanding season as a running back and quarterback in 1918, and his accomplishments were reported in the sports pages of the local paper.[5] He also played guard on the senior basketball team in his final year at high school. In addition, he played soccer and baseball and, after graduation, was shortstop on the Windsor team in the old Michigan-Ontario Baseball League, before it expanded to take in London, Flint, Grand Rapids, Hamilton, Kalamazoo, Bay City and Saginaw. One of his teammates was Charlie Gehringer, who later played for the Detroit Tigers from 1926 to 1942 and became one of the greatest second basemen ever in the American League.[6] In later life, David Croll became a first-class squash player.

Once out of high school, Croll was sufficiently astute to see the advantages of professional training. His uncle Isadore was a physician, and he toyed briefly with the idea of becoming a doctor. Instead, he chose law. This decision meant that he would have to meet the entrance requirements of Toronto's Osgoode Hall, which was then under the direction of the Law Society of Upper Canada. He would have to either earn a bachelor's degree from a university "in His Majesty's Dominions" or spend two years as a clerk in a lawyer's office. For reasons of economy, Croll's choice was obvious, and he sought employment with the law firm of Davis and Healy in Windsor. The senior partner and city solicitor, F. D. Davis, K.C., was a bachelor and very canny about money. The salary he offered was as meagre as the workload was heavy. Croll was kept busy morning to night serving papers, collecting agendas for city council meetings and carrying out the manifold duties of a lawyer's clerk.

As a law clerk, Croll became acquainted with T. J. Agar, K.C., partner in the Toronto law firm of Hughes and Agar, who came to Windsor on occasion in connection with insurance litigation. Working closely with Davis and Healy, Agar used Croll to interview witnesses and serve papers. Obviously impressed with the young man's initiative, he invited Croll to article in his Toronto offices. This invitation was a stroke of good fortune, since it was not easy for Jews to become articled to firms in Toronto, where prejudice effectively hindered their entry into some professional careers.

After his admission to the bar on 20 November 1924, Croll returned to Windsor to enter the law firm of Sheppard and Sheppard. His life as a poor law student behind him, his thoughts turned to establishing a family of his own. He had fallen in love with his former schoolmate Sarah Levin, usually known as Sally. The origin of their friendship, as Croll now admits, was her willingness to allow him to copy her homework in high school. Judging from their photographs, they made an attractive young couple indeed. Sally had graduated with a Bachelor of Education degree from the University of Michigan in Ann Arbor in 1924 and became a schoolteacher in Detroit. On 25 June 1925, they were married. At the time, Croll was making about thirty-five dollars a week, but within a couple of years, he was one of that favoured minority paying income tax to the federal government. He and Sally eventually produced three daughters: Eunice, born in 1927; Constance, born in 1929; and Sandra, born in 1934.

After a couple of years with Sheppard and Sheppard, Croll formed a partnership with two of his contemporaries, Leigh H. Snider and W. E. Kelly, and not long after, he established his own firm, where he employed Louis J. Brody, Milton Meretsky and his youngest brother, Cecil, who graduated from Osgoode Hall in 1932. In the late 1930s, with Cecil as a partner, the firm became Croll and Croll.

TWO

Breaking the Barriers

DAVID CROLL'S FIRST EXPOSURE TO POLITICS CAME WHEN his father took him to an outdoor rally during the 1911 federal election campaign. The main issue of the day was reciprocity with the United States, and on 10 September, a crowd of ten thousand from all over southwestern Ontario gathered in the bright sunshine in Ouellette Square to see and hear Canada's Liberal prime minister, Sir Wilfrid Laurier, concluding his tour of Ontario. Hillel Croll was a supporter of F. A. Dewar, the Liberal candidate in Essex North. In the election of 21 September, Dewar was defeated, as was the Liberal party nationally.

Croll's conversion to the Liberal cause came later. Like many of his generation, he was keenly interested in the radical reform ideas current immediately after World War I. Croll was particularly impressed by the Liberal convention of 1919, which featured the yeasty concepts of the new federal leader, Mackenzie King. A special section on labour and industry advocated the right to collective bargaining, the eight-hour day, unemployment insurance, sickness insurance and old age pensions. That these fields were all under provincial jurisdiction did nothing to diminish the enthusiasm of the faithful. Croll saw a talisman in the Liberal platform and became a party member in 1920.

He was blooded when he helped elect Francis Wellington Hay, M.P.P. for North Perth, leader of the Ontario Liberals. The background was this: Hartley Dewart had come to the end of his tether in early 1922, necessitating a provincial leadership convention, scheduled for 1 March in Foresters' Hall on College Street in Toronto. Apparently the Windsor Liberals could not afford to pay the travel costs of their quota of delegates. Someone remembered that young Croll was in Toronto studying law, so he was asked to stand in. F. Wellington Hay was elected on the first ballot. Unfortunately, he flashed across the sky like a small meteorite and does not seem to have left any mark on Ontario politics. Of more significance was the establishment of the separate Ontario Liberal Association. Croll was only a spear carrier at the convention, but the experience whetted his appetite for party politics.

By 1925, he was secretary of the Essex West Liberal Association, and his circle of political friends was growing rapidly. By the late 1920s, he was deeply involved in politics and played a major part in organizing the riding in the federal election of 1930.

During this period, Croll became friendly with W. F. Herman, the proprietor of the *Border Cities Star*. Herman, at one time the publisher of a Saskatoon newspaper, which he later sold to the Sifton interests, had come from the west in 1918 to take over the *Windsor Record*, which he renamed and transformed into an excellent, widely quoted newspaper with an influence beyond its circulation. The *Border Cities Star* was independent politically, but Herman was favourably impressed by Croll and encouraged him to become involved in the mayoralty campaigns in 1926 and 1928, in which Croll did canvassing and organizational work for Cecil Jackson, who was successful on both occasions.

When Mayor Jackson declined to run for re-election in 1930, Croll decided to try for the office himself. Although he was young, he was well known locally as an athlete, a lawyer and an active participant in a number of community organizations. Croll was a joiner, both for professional and for political reasons, and because he enjoyed associating with people. When he was at Osgoode Hall, he joined Pi Lambda Phi. Not long after he was called to the bar, he joined the Masons in Harmony Lodge No. 579 in Windsor (ultimately he would become a 32nd degree Mason in the Scottish Rite and a member of the Shrine). He also became a member of the Dr. Campbell Lodge 100F, the Goodfellows, the Maccabees, the Grotto and B'nai B'rith.

Croll had learned to take advantage of the polyglot character of the Windsor population when he worked to elect Jackson in 1926 and 1928, and he was quick to exploit this knowledge in his own campaign. He again approached the leaders of the various ethnic minorities for their support. Croll's identification with the Liberal party was also a big help in dealing with these groups, given their long-standing affinity with the party of Laurier and its immigration policies. Paul Martin recalled being

> ... one of the very few lawyers who actually gave open support to him. I campaigned for his election. I liked the way he was going to try and help people who needed relief in a city where unemployment was so high. I thought he was a natural politician. I liked his philosophy. [1]

When the dust settled late on the evening of 21 December, Croll emerged victorious, with a plurality of over a thousand votes in a five-man race. The *Border Cities Star* was ecstatic. It described Croll inaccurately as the first Jewish chief magistrate of a Canadian city[2] and led off its front page article with the following:

> This is the simple story of a little group of immigrants from the Ghetto of Moscow who arrived in the land of new hope one blustery day in the spring of the year 1906. Not one of them knew so much as a word of English, and they were nearly penniless. Undaunted, the family—father, mother and four sturdy sons, the eldest six years old—struck roots in the City of Windsor and started a slow climb upward through years of poverty which led the boys as they grew older to sell newspapers on the streets, to run errands for a hard-won dime and to fight for, and get, an education.[3]

The family had never been near Moscow, and in fact, Moscow had no ghetto. Neither was the family all that poor. But it was a touching tribute.

A few days after his election, Croll spoke to the Border Cities Chamber of Commerce, where he scoffed at the whispering campaign that his election expenses had been paid by Detroit bootleggers who were exporting liquor from Windsor across the river:

> In that campaign I neither asked nor did I receive favours. I worked hard and I had the support of a large number of faithful, energetic and capable workers for whose efforts I am deeply grateful. But... I think you will agree with me that my campaign was conducted fairly, was free from venom or personalities and resulted in a fair expression of opinion by the electors of Windsor.[4]

Indeed, he announced emphatically that Windsor would be a tough spot for gamblers and racketeers as long as he was mayor.

Obviously, Croll's success at the polls was not universally applauded. One of his opponents in the election, Welfare Commissioner Clyde W. Curry, claimed that not only had there been voting irregularities, but in addition Croll had disqualified himself by acting as legal counsel in a local assessment appeal. Croll issued a statement that he had retired from the case before nomination day. Curry, however, was successful in persuading city council to appoint a judicial inquiry, which dragged on for a long time before finally fizzling out. No doubt the welfare commissioner and his council cronies were more than a little exercised by the prospect of Croll's fulfilling his campaign promises to appoint people with central and eastern European backgrounds to various civic positions. This was in the days when, in Toronto, any jobs in the giving of City Hall were closed to anyone who was not an Orangeman.

December 1930 was a poor time to be elected to public office anywhere at any level. Windsor was especially vulnerable to the catastrophic economic decline that had been signalled by the dramatic fall in stock prices starting in October 1929. In part, the problems of the Border Cities stemmed from their heavy reliance on the automotive industry and the interdependence of Detroit and its economic satellite across the river.

The rapid growth of the automobile industry in Detroit during the 1920s had been parallelled in Windsor to take advantage of the British Preferential Tariff, which gave Canada an advantage in exporting to the British Empire. In 1929, total Canadian production amounted to 262,625 vehicles. By 1932, output had dropped to 60,816.[5] When Croll assumed office in January 1931, the inroads of the depression were very much in evidence. As if unemployment resulting from the decline of the Canadian auto industry were not bad enough, a large number of local residents worked across the river in Detroit, where their jobs were rapidly disappearing as well. For Windsor, this meant a sharply increased relief load, which may have amounted to as many as ten thousand individuals. The result was that unemployment in Windsor was probably worse and its welfare rolls longer than in any other place of comparable size in Canada. Croll and his city council did all they could to provide food, clothing and shelter for the needy, but their financial resources were strained to the limit and beyond.

It was a matter of principle with Croll to see anyone who came to his office with a problem. Many of the thousands who appeared at his door did not understand what was happening to them. Sometimes Croll could offer some help or solace, but often there was nothing he could do except make certain that he was there early each morning to oversee personally the operation of the soup kitchens and bread lines. This confrontation with the realities of unemployment, relief, sickness and poverty affected him profoundly and coloured his whole attitude towards Canada's social system. He became convinced that a good part of the privation could be alleviated through political action. His would be a long, uphill struggle, but at least he was pointed in the right direction.

Croll's first term as mayor of Windsor coincided with the dying days of the Great Experiment in the United States. The Eighteenth Amendment had turned Windsor into the undisputed bootlegging capital of North America. Phenomenal quantities of alcohol moved across the river from Windsor to Detroit. Boats with cargoes of liquor consigned to Mexico were unloaded midstream for transfer to closer destinations. Some of the Americans involved established residence in Windsor and often came to Croll's law office for advice and assistance in handling the technical aspects of these entirely legal purchases. Occasionally, Croll was invited to some of the better blind pigs in Detroit, where the entertainment and the whiskey were both first-rate.

Croll's open-door policy and his obvious concern for the needy during his first term as mayor increased his popularity with his constituents. He was so busy with his civic duties that his law practice suffered. With the bit in his teeth, however, he could not resist the challenge of the next election, scheduled for 5 December 1932. His opponents were his old antagonist, Clyde W. Curry, making a third bid for the job, and Joseph E. Lemaire. In his campaign, Croll pointed to his record over the last two years in reducing the city's bonded indebtedness by $1.5 million, while spending $500,000 on relief, and all this in the face of assessed property values that had fallen by $700,000. He also outlined a plan for a five-year moratorium on the principal payments on the city's debts, an extension of debentures over a thirty- to thirty-five-year period and a reduction of interest rates.

When the results of the election were announced, Croll was an easy winner. His plurality of 7,082 was the largest in the history of the city, with a majority in every one of the 136 polls. In a magnanimous victory speech, Croll said, in part: "The victory belongs to the people. It is their victory, not my victory. I am their servant. They have shown their belief that responsible government must be maintained in this city."[6]

The *Border Cities Star* commented that "it was a wonderful victory for as fine, as sincere, as conscientious a man as Windsor has ever known" and then expanded on this theme in a longer editorial:

We have spoken of the personal tribute to Mayor Croll. It was indeed wonderful, one to stir the heart of every man and every woman who believes in the gospel of fair play, human kindness, racial and religious freedom and tolerance. The people gave their answer to those who opposed the Mayor because he happens to be a Jew, because he happens to have been born in Russia, because he has lifted himself up from obscurity to the highest position in the city. The Star is exultant over this phase of the election. It glories in the fact that Windsor has once more demonstrated that it has no use for bigotry, for attempted social distinctions that rank with superciliousness, for attempts to set class against class, race against race, faith against faith.[7]

This tribute was undoubtedly written by Star publisher W. F. Herman.

Croll's life continued to be dominated by the dreary subjects of unemployment, relief and municipal solvency. In April 1933, he attended a conference on the problems of local relief administration. One resolution favouring the British system of cash relief caused him to speak at length, arguing that the morale of the people on relief was indeed being broken by standardization. He claimed that a person wearing relief clothing was easily identified. He had heard of children who were ashamed to go to school because their shoes showed that they were on relief. He urged that Ontario also adopt a system of cash relief, as did a majority of the other delegates, but they would have to wait for the election of a new government at Queen's Park.

Croll also understood the importance of even the smallest gestures when dealing with welfare recipients. Shortly before one Christmas, he ordered the Windsor welfare department to give every family on its rolls a turkey. In December 1933, turkeys cost sixteen to twenty-five cents a pound, so the extra cost was not great relative to the city's total relief bill. As a practical expression of sentiment, however, this act was a ray of hope and light to thousands of poor people for whom such rays were all too rare.

In the late spring of 1933, Croll became involved in a political storm that brought him into sharp conflict with the provincial government and splashed his name over the pages of most of the newspapers in Ontario. The controversy arose over the back-to-the-land movement. With the onset of the depression, a shift of population to fertile pockets of land in northern Ontario seemed to offer a promising, if limited, solution to the aggravated problems of unemployment and relief in urban areas. The relief land-settlement scheme fell under the jurisdiction of the provincial Department of Lands and Forests, which provided guidance to the settlers through local relief land-settlement committees.

When a number of families from the Windsor area who had moved north in 1932 sent back distressing reports, Croll, along with Harry E. Gignac of the Windsor Board of Control, a Conservative, decided to conduct a personal, bipartisan investigation. The two men travelled by automobile to visit twenty-one families in the Kapuskasing area and found them living in uniformly deplorable conditions and close to starvation.[8] As soon as they returned, Croll convinced the Windsor City Council to vote a small supplement to their meagre monthly provincial dole of ten dollars a family. The council also agreed that a delegation would call on William Finlayson, the minister of lands and forests, to ask for an increase in the pitiful scale of relief provided by his department, that settlers be moved from unsuitable farms and that those former local families not fit for the rigours of life in northern Ontario be sent back to Windsor.[9] When the dispute simmered down, it became clear that despite the soundness of the basic concept underlying resettlement, the administrative structure of inspection and counselling was inadequate. Major reforms were introduced, but earlier public enthusiasm for the back-to-the-land movement had waned.

Late in 1933, Croll became entangled in a bitter, front page controversy over the operations of the Windsor Children's Aid Society shelter for orphan children. Charges of child abuse had been made against Magdalene Strang, the matron of this institution, and her sister, Catherine, who acted as her assistant. Croll, a member of the local Children's Aid Society, had been told of irregular happenings at the shelter, some reminiscent of Dotheboys Hall in *Nicholas Nickleby*. In addition to the claims of mistreatment, however, there had been several deaths, which raised questions about the adequacy of medical care.

Despite indications that the Strang sisters were temperamentally unsuited to care for a group of underprivileged children, there was a difference of view among members of the local Children's Aid Society about their behaviour and competence. Certainly, the Misses Strang were skilled at public relations, and a sizable community in Windsor was convinced that they were kind and caring. Croll, knowing he would be vilified to some degree for questioning their charity, could have backed away from the problem, but felt compelled to intervene. He armed himself with sixteen affidavits, mostly from employees or former employees of the shelter, and appeared before the provincial Children's Aid Society in Toronto on 9 November 1933. Some of the charges included forced feedings, beatings, attempting to stick a child's head in a toilet and the indiscriminate use of bichloride of mercury (corrosive sublimate) for topical application and as a general disinfectant. It was claimed that often the children were given dry bread for supper with nothing to drink. It was also alleged that it was usual for fifteen-year-old girls to bathe fifteen-year-old boys, although it was not stated whether they objected to this practice. As Croll said at the hearing, "The charges are serious, almost unbelievable, in some instances."[10]

In his presentation, Croll said that because certain members of the local and provincial Children's Aid Societies had a protective attitude towards the Strang sisters, he would ask the Ontario government to name an independent body to conduct an inquiry. Consequently, he turned over copies of his affidavits and a transcript of the proceedings before the provincial Children's Aid Society to W. G. Martin, the minister of public welfare in the Henry government, who immediately dispatched an inspector to Windsor.

Subsequently, on 17 November, Milton Arthur Sorsoleil was appointed a commissioner under the Public Inquiries Act:

1. TO inquire into the conduct, management and administration of the Children's Shelter at Windsor, Ontario, and all matters in connection therewith, or incidental thereto.
2. TO report upon the evidence and facts brought out by the investigation.[11]

Sorsoleil was the deputy minister of public welfare, an ex-schoolteacher, a prominent layman in the United Church and a Tory. He began his investigations almost immediately, assisted by I. A. Humphries, deputy attorney general, acting as counsel. Croll's allegations had stirred provincewide interest, and Sorsoleil's hearings were covered in detail by the press.

Altogether, the inquiry heard ninety witnesses and continued hearings until well on in January 1934. In early February, Sorsoleil delivered his report to W. G. Martin, who released it to the public with the following comments:

I am in complete agreement with the findings of the commission and shall issue instructions immediately that all the recommendations be carried out. . . . The Windsor investigation, which has provoked such widespread attention, will have a salutary effect by way of quickening the sense of responsibility on the part of all boards and officials entrusted with the responsibility of supervising the lives of unfortunate and under-privileged children placed under their care.[12]

Croll's charges of mismanagement and dereliction had been substantiated, and the report recommended the dismissal of the Misses Strang, along with M. R. Winters, superintendent of the institution.

Naturally, Windsor's troubled financial position continued to absorb much of Croll's time. By 1933, the Border Cities were faced with insolvency as a result of falling tax revenues and mounting relief costs. In 1934, out of a total population of nearly 100,000, an average of 28,636 persons received relief throughout the year. The only area in which there was not a problem was housing; the city could boast accommodation for 107,000 persons because of the exodus of those seeking work in greener fields. Default on the Windsor debentures was unavoidable, and Croll wanted to make an arrangement with the bondholders that would permit city council to control its own finances, subject to the recommendations of a financial adviser. Croll also wanted to refinance Windsor's debt. Unfortunately, the Ontario government intervened under the provisions of the Municipal Act and assigned control of the city's finances to a committee of supervisors. Similar committees were appointed in a number of municipalities, but the opposition in Windsor and elsewhere was so pronounced that the provincial government was forced to back down.[13]

Another feature of the depression in Ontario was rural unrest, in part a legacy of the 1920s. The farmers resented the Henry government's encouragement of industry and recalled with nostalgia the time when their political power was unchallenged. The ability of the farmers to directly control the political process may have come unravelled, but their votes were not to be ignored. The proportion of the rural population in Ontario was falling, as the table below shows, but it was still substantial in 1931 and potentially decisive in more ridings than mere population ratios might suggest.

Year	Percentage rural population
1891	61
1901	57
1911	47
1921	42
1931	39

All this was very important to the young man who had taken over as leader of the Liberal party in Ontario in December 1930. Indeed, Mitchell Frederick Hepburn's political career had begun with the United Farmers of Ontario, and his attachment to the land continued all his life. He was so completely at home making political speeches dotted with pungent witticism to his fellow farmers that Arthur Roebuck, minister of labour in Hepburn's cabinet, once described him as "the comedy kid of the back concessions."[14] From the outset, Hepburn attacked the Conservatives and their works without mercy, much to the delight not only of his rural audiences but also to many city dwellers who had been dispossessed by the depression. His biographer outlined Hepburn's plans:

Immediately on taking office the Liberals would slash the administrative costs of government by 50 per cent; all those superfluous boards and commissions (no less than 23 of them) that drew down juicy salaries and cluttered up office space would be abolished; high-priced supernumeraries would be summarily sacked. . . . [15]

David Croll and Mitch Hepburn were friends. Croll had encouraged him to seek the Liberal leadership and in turn was asked by Hepburn to run in the next provincial election. Although no public commitment was made in advance, Croll was an obvious choice as Hepburn's minister of public welfare. As mayor of Windsor, Croll had introduced many innovative features in dealing with relief and welfare and was the logical person to take on the thorny job of administering the related issues faced by the province, should the Liberals form a government.

That Croll was Jewish did not deter Hepburn, though he did check with the party organization. About a year before the Ontario election of 1934, Mackenzie King wrote in his diary:

Tonight I had Mr. & Mrs. J. I. Frieman [A. J. Freiman] from Meaches Lake (to dinner). He had asked to see me about a letter Crowell [Croll?] of Windsor had written him which said Hepburn had promised him a portfolio in the Ont. Govt., subject to Arthur Hardy's approval. He wanted my advice or reaction. I told him by all means to see Hardy if he approved the idea and thought Crowell [sic] a good man.[16]

At this time Freiman was president of the Canadian Zionist Organization. For some reason, he did not reply to Croll's letter.

Years later Croll said in an interview:

I never dreamt that he [Hepburn] had the guts to put me in the cabinet and I never realized the opposition he'd get against putting me in, not because I was Dave Croll but because I was a Jew. And he once told me where the opposition came from and I was a little surprised that he did but there was no opposition once I got in.[17]

Although he did not reveal it in the interview, the arguments against Croll's selection appear to have come from Percy Parker, Frank O'Connor (later senator) and other members of the inner circle of the Liberal party in Toronto.

Once the writs were issued for the provincial election, Croll was named the Liberal candidate in Windsor-Walkerville at a nominating meeting of over two thousand party members. Hepburn was the only outside politician to speak on his behalf during the campaign, although Croll made appeals in support of the Liberal candidates in Chatham, London, St. Thomas, Kincardine and other neighbouring communities, where he had been assigned responsibility by Hepburn for the supervision of candidates and political fund raising.

Croll's own campaign focussed on the positive measures he would attempt if elected, particularly in welfare and housing. He concentrated on bread and butter issues and urged his band of candidates to do the same. On the contentious issue of drink, Croll was a "wet" and supported the sale of beer by the glass. Hepburn's campaign, however, was marked by continual attacks on the Henry government for extravagance, corruption and waste. There was a great fuss about the use of government automobiles, which Hepburn promised to auction off if he were elected. Nearly every day, Hepburn had new charges of some kind against the government, and whatever their merits, they made good copy. His vigour seemed boundless. During the campaign, he travelled over six thousand miles, mainly by car, and made seventy speeches, sometimes four or five a day.

In Windsor, the *Border Cities Star* gave Croll its enthusiastic support. About two weeks before the election, W. F. Herman, in a lengthy boxed statement, wrote an encomium of Croll and all his works. Herman did not spare the superlatives:

But my object in writing this is to pay a humble tribute to Dave Croll. Not that he needs any words of mine to ensure his election. He will take care of that task himself.

I have known Dave for a considerable time. Long before he gave any hint to me that he had political aspirations he was a welcome visitor to the Star office. He is one of the few men who have ever been able to go into a newspaper office at any time of the day or night and enjoy almost proprietary rights, without abusing them.

When Dave decided to be a candidate for the mayoralty he came and asked me what I thought of the idea. Frankly, I didn't think he could win and I gave him my reason for saying so. He thought he could and gave quite convincing proof for confidence in his success. . . .

As we said at the beginning of this little article, Dave does not need any words of mine to help him along in this campaign. Nevertheless, so close has our friendship been and so great is my admiration for him that I feel constrained to put these few words in print. With his sympathetic feeling toward his fellow-men; with an ever-ready desire to help those who are not in a position to help themselves; and with his ability, his integrity and his remarkable industry, Dave Croll should go far.

I will make it even stronger than that—Dave Croll WILL go far.[18]

Herman's observations were summarized in an editorial in the Toronto *Globe* on 8 June, to which the *Globe* added:

Mr. Herman is known as an excellent judge of men. Without saying so, he has sized up Mayor Croll as the sort of man needed these days in public administration. He is the sort required at Queen's Park to do for the Province what he has accomplished for Windsor.

The Conservatives had grown old and tired in office, and it is not surprising that they were soundly defeated. When the final tallies were in, the Liberals had won sixty-six seats and the Conservatives seventeen. There were three Progressives and one survivor of the United Farmers of Ontario, but these four were effectively Liberal supporters. Hepburn and his organizers had been fairly confident of solid rural support, but they entertained some uncertainty about the vote in Toronto and the other big cities. In the event, these doubts proved groundless, and there was joy in the Liberal camp on 19 June. The Conservative regime had ended decisively, its fate like that of many other governments determined by the heartbreaking economic malaise of the early 1930s.

On his home ground, David Croll did very nicely. His emphasis on welfare and related issues proved to be a sound strategy in a riding that had both urban and suburban components and an economic and ethnic potpourri. His plurality was 5,324, the second largest in the election. In response to a message of congratulations from Mackenzie King, Croll replied:

> It was a source of very great pleasure to me to receive your very kind wire of Wednesday. I want to express my appreciation of the same. It was indeed a splendid victory in Ontario and a triumph for the entire Liberal party.[19]

True to his promise, Mitch Hepburn invited Croll to join his new government as a member of the executive council and minister of public welfare. This was a fitting tribute to both Croll's political ability and his demonstrated administrative capacity. When he was sworn in on 10 July 1934, it was a noteworthy event. For one thing, he was the first Jew to become a cabinet minister in Canada; for another, he was the youngest minister in the British Empire at the time.[20]

The swearing-in ceremony, however, was attended by a novel problem of protocol. All the members of the cabinet except Croll were summoned into the drawing room at Chorley Park to be sworn in by the lieutenant governor, Dr. H. A. Bruce. Croll was left to cool his heels in an anteroom for a considerable time and could not understand the delay. It was not until some years later that he learned what had happened. The lieutenant governor asked how to swear in a Jew, but no one knew. The clerk then called Ottawa to obtain the advice of the federal experts, but they had no experience either. At this point, it was necessary to call London for guidance. The response was that any binding oath was satisfactory. Finally, Croll was called in to take his oath of office on the Old Testament (King James version).[21]

THREE

Minister of Good Works

NOT EVERYBODY WAS ENTHRALLED BY THE NEW PREMIER. Shortly after Hepburn was named leader of the Ontario Liberals, J. E. Atkinson, publisher of the *Toronto Daily Star*, observed to Arthur Roebuck, "I do not like him; I do not like his habits and I do not like the company he keeps."[1] The editorial in the paper after Hepburn's victory appears to bear Atkinson's stamp:

> Mr. Hepburn has courage which verges on recklessness. His success in yesterday's election may be attributed in no small part to his elimination of the liquor question as an issue between the parties by declaring his intention to proclaim the wine and beer act that was put through by the Henry government. He worked himself almost into exhaustion during the campaign and his pungent and humorous presentation of Liberal arguments seemed to impress popular audiences.
>
> In some quarters Mr. Hepburn is regarded as only a "wisecracker" and in others as a man without fixed principles. But it is scarcely likely he would have gained so rapidly in public

favour if he did not possess some of the qualifications that mark the statesman. He has ability, a ready smile and a friendly manner and does not put on "side." He puts people at their ease and disarms criticism by his human-ness. Not improbably he will become Ontario's best-liked premier. But for lasting success he will have to depend upon the soundness of his judgment in choosing his ministers and shaping his policies.[2]

Hepburn and Croll were kindred spirits in their early associations. They were close both politically and personally, and well before the election Croll had been advising Hepburn on political issues, particularly the temperance problem. In a letter before the election, Croll, somewhat prematurely, had even proposed the sale of beer in grocery stores.[3] Indeed, when Hepburn discovered that Croll's name had been omitted from the list of new K.C.'s presented for his signature, he balked, saying, in effect, that unless Dave Croll was on the list, he would not sign it. It was explained that the standards of the Law Society of Upper Canada required that a lawyer be in practice for ten years before being awarded this distinction and Croll was one year short. Hepburn would not stir. A compromise resulted in the inclusion of Croll's name, although it was agreed that he would not be formally called until the following year.

Hepburn's success was good news for the federal Liberals in the general election of 1935. Croll was called to Port Arthur to speak on behalf of a newcomer to Canadian politics, C. D. Howe. And much against his will, he also travelled to Winnipeg North to help C. S. Booth, who was the Liberal candidate running against A. A. Heaps for the Co-operative Commonwealth Federation (CCF) and Tim Buck for the Communists. Mackenzie King wanted Heaps, who had held the seat since 1925, defeated, but Heaps was Jewish and Croll did not relish the job of trying to damage him politically. He begged to be excused. King would have none of it and appealed to Hepburn, who brought appropriate pressure to bear. Finally, Croll felt obliged to conform.

J. A. Cherniack, a Winnipeg lawyer who supported Heaps, wrote to H. M. Caiserman, the executive secretary of the Canadian Jewish Congress, on 15 September 1935, about a month before the election, that

> Hon. David Croll, Ontario Minister of Health [sic] is rumoured to be coming to support the Liberal candidate opposing A. A. Heaps. Any threat to Heaps, one of the three Jewish Members in Commons, would be regrettable.[4]

Cherniack also wrote to Croll intimating that the majority of Winnipeg Jews supported Heaps and resented Croll's interference.[5] Croll looks back on his role with regret, but it would have been a dereliction of his political duty to refuse the request of Hepburn and King. As things turned out, Heaps was successful in the election, no doubt helped in his campaign by the five hundred dollars that Croll and Sam Factor, Liberal M.P. for Spadina, acting together, sent in expiation.

Croll found that being a cabinet minister had an immediate effect on his lifestyle. He was the owner of a 1934 Ford V-8 sedan, but W. F. Herman, who was a man of means, convinced Croll that it was beneath the dignity of his office to drive around in such a plebeian car. Hepburn had made a campaign promise to auction off the official limousines of cabinet ministers, so there was no hope that a grateful government would come to his rescue. Finally, Croll yielded to Herman's notion of propriety and acquired a handsome black La Salle sedan, one of the luxury automobiles produced by General Motors in the 1930s, although he always felt slightly uncomfortable travelling in such style when his principal responsibility was to look after the jobless.

The big question, of course, was where to find enough money to provide relief to the province's unemployed and destitute, a problem confounded by successive federal governments, which, regardless of party, disavowed responsibility on constitutional grounds. The Conservative position was stated in the early 1920s by Prime Minister Arthur Meighen in reply to a plea from the Winnipeg civic authorities:

> Unemployment relief is purely a function of municipal government, and the Municipalities of Canada cannot expect the Federal Government to undertake any responsibility, financial or otherwise, in connection with it.[6]

Some years later, the Liberal position was given voice in the notoriously partisan statement of Prime Minister Mackenzie King:

> With respect to giving moneys out of the federal treasury to any Tory government in this country for these alleged unemployment purposes, with these governments situated as they are today, with policies diametrically opposed to those of this government, I would not give them a five-cent piece.[7]

Although the federal government did its best to resist supplications from the provinces, the pressures created by the urgent need of so many individual Canadians kept building. The following estimates may be imprecise, but the federal outlays for relief, including public works and agricultural relief, showed a steady upward trend:

Year	$ million
1931	20
1932	90
1933	95
1934	105
1935	155
1936	170
	635

The total was broken down into these categories:

Type of aid	$ million
public works	211
agricultural relief and aid	42
direct and miscellaneous	361[8]

Fortunately, Croll was familiar with the problem of welfare and unemployment relief from his experience in Windsor. He inherited a dreary situation at the provincial level. In 1931–32, direct relief in Ontario was over $25 million, with one-half the cost being borne by the federal and the provincial governments and the balance being paid by the municipalities. The municipalities, however, could no longer bear their share, as Croll explained to the Ontario legislature on 4 April 1935:

The plain fact remains that it is the cost of relief which has been forcing municipalities into bankruptcy. Already saddled with heavy debenture debts, they are finding it impossible to carry on their necessary services, pay their interest and principal, and in addition carry the new and unexpected burden of relief costs. It is not fair that they should have to carry any considerable portion of the relief, because its cost imposes an impossible load of taxation on land and buildings, a load which was never contemplated when the relationship of municipality, Province and Dominion was established.[9]

Every province looked to Ottawa for succour, but the federal politicians were still very cautious. In 1932–33, Ottawa's contribution to relief for the entire country was only $35 million. This was, of course, in addition to loans of $17 million to the western provinces to help them pay their share of relief costs.[10] The federal minister of labour estimated that 1.3 million Canadians were on relief in March 1933, out of a total population of roughly 10 million.[11] A year later the figure was still 1.2 million.[12] And these statistics probably conceal the true magnitude of the problem, since it was impossible to identify people who were dependent on charity from private persons, churches or relatives.

The underlying philosophy of publicly funded relief was based on the experience of centuries in Britain. The English poor law, although reformed from time to time, had one fundamental principle: to make relief a bare substitute for starvation. Historically, conditions in the poorhouses and the workhouses were so miserable that almost any wage or drudgery seemed an acceptable alternative. It is astonishing that many otherwise responsible people have continued to this very day to advance this same philosophy. Certainly there was something brutally primitive in the strictures on relief recipients in Ontario in the 1930s. Author Joseph Schull describes a few of the indignities endured by those on welfare:

The recipient of a relief voucher had first to surrender his liquor permit and his licence plates and driver's licence if he had managed to keep his car. In most cases the telephone was disconnected. Nothing was allowed to the man for cigarettes or tobacco or haircuts or a newspaper; still less to the woman for such frivolities as lipstick.[13]

Soon after his appointment as minister, Croll encountered the intransigence of the federal government. On 27 July 1934, Hepburn left for Ottawa with Croll hard on his heels to attend upon Prime Minister R. B. Bennett, who had convened a federal/provincial conference to discuss the burden of relief costs. The provincial premiers were alarmed that the federal government proposed to withdraw direct relief. Bennett, not content with merely shifting the burden, took the opportunity to lecture the provinces on their waste and lamentable administrative methods. Ontario, he said, was wealthy enough to look after its own financial problems.

It was hard for Croll, who had faced the problem at close quarters in Windsor, to agree with Bennett's charge that relief administered by the municipalities had become a racket and that the relief lists were being padded with the aged, the infirm, even children. The federal government had decided that it could not tolerate such sloppiness where federal money was involved and that from then on the provinces would be given an unconditional grant based on need. The Ontario position was that $1 million a month was essential, not counting federally funded relief works. Hepburn and Croll were told that the allotment to Ontario would be $500,000 a month, beginning immediately. Faced with Hepburn's protests, Bennett agreed to provide $1 million for each of the next two months to enable the new government to review its situation, but any unspent balance was to be refunded to Ottawa. Hepburn refused to agree, and he and Croll returned to Toronto.

When they came back to renew the negotiations three weeks later, the Ontario contingent[14] repeated its earlier request but in the end had to settle for $1 million a month for

August and September and $600,000 a month thereafter, until May 1935. There was to be no further federal aid for relief work projects. Ontario was not alone in its disappointment. Grant Dexter wrote:

> The immediate consequence of this new deal has been to stir up the deepest resentment on the part of the provincial governments. To be told that they are solely responsible for a problem that, patently, is beyond their financial capacity to cope with, to be put off with cash handouts conceived in a niggardly, ungenerous way, has been exasperating in the extreme.[15]

In the summer of 1935, the financial burden of relief continued to harass Hepburn in his capacity as premier and provincial treasurer. Sixty per cent of provincial revenues were now needed to pay for the relief of 400,000 otherwise destitute people.[16] He announced that effective 1 January 1936, the province would no longer pay two thirds of the cost of direct relief but would substitute per capita grants to the municipalities based on their ability to pay.

Federally, Bennett was defeated in the autumn of 1935, with no small help from Hepburn, Croll and the rest of the Ontario Liberals. Twenty-four seats in the province were added to the 1930 Liberal victory column for a grand total of fifty-six out of a possible eighty-two. The new government of Mackenzie King pledged a more enlightened attitude towards relief, but the extent of its generosity was still uncertain. In December 1935, Prime Minister King summoned the provincial premiers to another federal/provincial conference to deal, in part, with relief issues. Hepburn and Croll proposed that the federal government take over three quarters of the cost of direct relief for employable people, leaving the unemployable to the care of the provinces and the municipalities. Although this proposal was not acceptable to Norman Rogers, King's minister of labour, on the grounds that it would drastically increase federal relief costs, Ontario's monthly grant was increased from $600,000 to $1,040,000.

In the spring of 1936, however, there was a falling out. Rogers decided to reduce this amount to $892,500, effective 1 April, on the grounds that the Ontario economy was showing signs of recovery and that the number of individuals on relief was dropping. In June, it was further arbitrarily reduced to $803,250.[17] Hepburn, in retaliation, refused to have anything to do with a forthcoming meeting of the National Liberal Federation and in effect cut off Ontario party funds to the federal Liberals. This move was related to a long-simmering personal feud between Hepburn and Mackenzie King, which was to poison relations between Ottawa and Queen's Park for years.

Whereas the negotiations with Ottawa were always important, it was up to Croll to face the voters within the province. Early in April 1935, he outlined three essential features of Ontario's welfare policy: (a) relief administration should be rationalized and relief scales equalized; (b) a genuine effort should be made to provide the unemployed with enough work to earn at least the necessities of life so that they would feel they were paying their way; (c) all possible means should be tried to provide relief in cash and not in a multiplicity of vouchers.

Croll noted that the scale of relief was a hodgepodge. Standards varied appreciably even in adjacent areas. In one place the weekly allowance for food for a family on relief was three dollars, and in another place not fifty miles away a family of the same size was receiving six dollars. Some municipalities were providing shelter costs for home owners in arrears on their taxes and others were not. Lack of co-ordination, which was due in part to lack of supervisory staff, was one source of inequity. Some of the variations occurred because of unscrupulous or venal municipal politicians. To minimize all this,

Croll introduced a scheme whereby the supervisory unit of administration was the county rather than the municipality.

One novel move in the direction of uniformity was the introduction of a standard scale of cash relief for food. Part of the scale was:

Family size	Monthly allowance ($)
I	16.89
2	29.59
3	36.53
4	43.16
5	49.53
etc.	etc.

Croll claimed that these allowances were the highest in Canada.

He was sensitive to the morale problems of the unemployed and took steps to eliminate the line-ups at relief offices, contending that queues led to discontent and humiliation. As an alternative, he introduced visits by social or relief workers so that interviews could take place privately. His motivation was doubtless admirable, but this scheme also gave the social worker the opportunity to do a little discreet snooping to see if anyone was bending the rules.

As noted earlier, one of the recurring problems throughout the depression was the suspicion that relief recipients were dishonest and too often fell into the Elizabethan category of "sturdy beggars." Croll was faced with the perennial issue of welfare frauds, but he also recognized that particular groups exaggerated chiselling for their own purposes. Croll was an old hand in this field and adopted a rigid policy of eliminating freeloaders, but was scrupulous in making sure that needy relief recipients did not suffer. From a political point of view, the course of wisdom was to be stern and righteous.

In August 1934, Croll announced a major overhaul of the

relief system, giving municipalities the choice between using cash relief or food vouchers and rent orders. He laid down the rule however, that any able-bodied man receiving cash relief was obliged to give the municipality or province in return an equivalent value in physical labour or other work. His policy was "relief to workers, nothing to shirkers."[18] This was not primarily an economy measure, nor was it an attempt to impose outmoded concepts on those receiving relief. Rather it represented a profound personal conviction about the work ethic, as Croll explained to the Ontario House:

> One of the dangers which I long ago saw with disquiet and fear in unemployment relief as it is being dispensed in this Province, was that able-bodied men were being given rations, shelter, clothing and other commodities without being required to make any return. Who will seriously attempt to deny that this was detrimental to anyone's morale. Something for nothing is a dangerous creed. . . . [19]

It was not surprising that on 15 September 1936, Croll announced that all those on relief in large urban centres would have to register with the newly formed National Employment Commission.[20] Croll had also had the opportunity to see the British system in operation when at the suggestion of Norman Rogers, he undertook a trip to England, Scotland and Wales in the summer of 1935. Croll and Rogers had become fast friends when the latter, an economist on the faculty of Queen's University, had carried out a number of research projects for Croll. (Subsequently, Rogers resigned from Queen's and ran successfully in the federal election of 13 October 1935.) When Mackenzie King appointed him minister of labour, he and Croll shared an even greater community of interest until his tragic death in 1940. In Britain, Croll visited the coal-mining areas of Wales and the industrial areas of the

Midlands and got as far north as Glasgow. He found it an exhilarating and invaluable time, and he learned a great deal. His only problem was that when he wanted to continue on to visit the Soviet Union, his hosts in the British Ministry of Labour vetoed the idea on the grounds that if he went to the land of his birth he might have difficulty in returning. His visit to Mother Russia would have to wait (a full thirty years, as it turned out).

Croll also introduced badly needed reforms in the provision of medical care to persons on relief in 1935. The system Croll had inherited from the Ontario Conservatives was far from ideal. Under it, the doctor of a welfare patient received one-half his normal fee per visit and 12.5 per cent of the cost of any medicines prescribed, subject to the restriction that no doctor could earn more than one hundred dollars a month from treating those on relief. Croll devised an alternative program in co-operation with the Ontario Medical Association (OMA) under which the complete cost of medical care for those on relief was defrayed by the province. In brief, the government paid one dollar a month for every person on relief, including dependent family members, to the OMA, which, in turn, paid the doctors for their services. This new system worked so well that Ontario became a model for a number of jurisdictions in North America.

Once Croll had dealt with the broader issues, he turned his attention to the problems of special disadvantaged groups. He sponsored an amendment to the Mothers' Allowance Act to include mothers with one child. Previously, mothers in need had to have at least two children before they could qualify for assistance. Another significant step forward was Croll's promotion of foster parenting. Children were taken from shelters and orphanages and placed in foster homes under the supervision of welfare workers and the Children's Aid Society. Croll also brought a number of professional social workers into his ministry to provide a continual review of the conditions among families on relief and closed down the worn-out, unsuitable buildings in Toronto that were used as a municipal reformatory for juvenile offenders.

In early 1937, he proposed that the province assume the entire cost of mothers' allowances as well as the municipal share of old age pensions. Previously, the provincial government and the municipalities had shared the cost of mothers' allowances equally, whereas the cost of old age pensions was shared by the three levels of government: federal, 75 per cent; provincial, 15 per cent; municipalities, 10 per cent. Croll rationalized that those earning enough to pay income taxes (the wealthy) should bear the cost of social services as far as possible to reduce the burden of real estate taxation.[21]

Croll was responsible as well for the 1935 campaign to promote the adoption of babies in Ontario. There was a barrage of publicity about his brain wave, "Adopt-a-Baby Week," the last week in May. The twenty-eighth of May was the first birthday of the Dionne quintuplets, and the adoption campaign was a celebration of this event. Croll issued a press statement, saying in part, "Everyone approves of identifying with the rejoicing over the quintuplets' first birthday with a remembrance of children who are not famous, but forgotten."[22] There were pictures of some of the more attractive of these adoptable children in the *Toronto Daily Star*, and people were invited to submit their adoption applications directly to Croll. His goal was to place about nine thousand of the children then in shelters or foster homes. There was an enormous demand, and the Children's Aid Society had to increase its staff to handle the workload. Even Hepburn was caught up in the enthusiasm and adopted a two-and-a-half-year-old boy and later a daughter.[23]

The birth of the Dionne quintuplets on 28 May 1934 had been a rare event. Only two previous cases of quintuplets had been recorded in medical history, and in neither case did the babies live longer than two months. Although it was not immediately evident, the unusual aspect of the Canadian phenomenon, however, was that the Dionne children were identical, not fraternal. Their parents, Oliva and Elzire Dionne, lived in Corbeil, near Callander, in northern Ontario, about 10 kilometres from North Bay. By good fortune, they had the services of Dr. Allan Roy Dafoe, a country doctor, who managed to keep these premature babies alive in the most primitive of circumstances until other professional help and specialized equipment became available. Worldwide interest in the quintuplets soared as the international press featured minutely detailed accounts of their progress and welfare.

Their parents, simple people living in rural poverty, were overwhelmed by instant fame. Consequently, the possibility of commercial exploitation was a threat to the babies, and anything that might impair their chances of survival became a vicarious concern to a great many people as well as to the government of Ontario. In his innocence, possibly tinged with cupidity, Oliva Dionne entered into a contract with a small-time American promoter, Ivan Spear, to display the quintuplets at the 1934 Chicago World's Fair.

This scheme was called to the attention of I. A. Humphries, the Ontario deputy attorney general, by W. H. Alderson, head of the Canadian Red Cross in northern Ontario. Humphries, in turn, telephoned Croll, who called a meeting of his legal advisers to consider the problem. One of them, Herbert Leopold Cummings, later law clerk of the Legislative Assembly and deputy minister of municipal affairs, suggested that the children be declared wards of the Crown. Because Croll was sensitive to possible public reaction against a Jew's taking Roman Catholic children from their parents, he took this proposal to Hepburn and suggested that the premier take charge. Hepburn declined. Instead, he instructed Croll to take this responsibility. Consequently, Croll sent his representative, Alf Gray, head of the Inspection Division of the Department of Public Welfare, to Corbeil. Gray arrived a day or two before the scheduled departure of the children for Chicago and assumed complete control of the situation and the quintuplets. All travel plans were cancelled. In the meantime, Arthur Roebuck, the attorney general, acting as *parens patriae*, obtained a court order in North Bay declaring the babies wards of the province and effectively nullifying the Oliva Dionne/Ivan Spear "perfidious contract."[24] A special hospital was built for the children, which Croll opened on 14 September 1934.

There were dissenting voices, however. The original contract with the Chicago promoter provided that 7 per cent of the gate was to go to Father Daniel Routhier, the Dionnes' parish priest, "as personal manager of the family." Father Routhier, among other things, stated publicly that the provincial guardianship arrangements were not binding. Fortunately, his opinion proved of little consequence, since his superiors saw to his prompt transfer.

As events turned, the mountain came to Mohammed; it was estimated that 500,000 visitors came to see the quintuplets in 1936. Croll had also been instrumental in building new roads in the area and in securing government grants to expand the facilities of nearby hotels and motels to accommodate the hordes of tourists. The children were an advertiser's dream, and within a short time everyone involved, except the babies, wanted to share the bonanza. Some type of permanent guardianship was needed, and the responsibility for this again was turned over to Croll as minister of public welfare. He steered legislation through the Ontario House, making himself a special guardian and empowering the lieutenant governor in council to appoint others.[25] Fortunately, Croll was able to second Joseph Sedgwick, a senior solicitor in the attorney general's office, to look after the complex affairs of the Dionne family and Dafoe. Sedgwick became, in his own words, "the legal and business manager of the quintuplets." He negotiated a deal that was to give the Newspaper Enterprises Association (NEA) copyright on all photographs of the children, and this organization was very helpful in maintaining reasonably decorous standards of advertising and promotion. An agency of the *Toronto Daily Star* acquired the exclusive Canadian rights from the NEA.

When Darryl Zanuck, the Hollywood producer, initiated plans to make a motion picture about the quintuplets, Sedgwick and Croll sought the advice of Mary Pickford on the intricacies of motion picture rights. She was not only a Canadian by birth but also an experienced businesswoman. The gist of her counsel was to get the money rather than any contingent benefits. The project advanced rapidly, and in 1936, the film *Country Doctor* appeared with Jean Hersholt playing the part of Dr. Dafoe.

Croll flew to Hollywood for a private screening of the movie early in November 1936. A picture in the *Windsor Star* shows him emerging from the aircraft to be greeted by the actress Virginia Field. There followed a round of parties, studio visits, luncheons and lavish dinners. This display of hospitality was the least the Hollywood moguls could do for Croll, whose co-operation had been essential to the financial success of their movie. Croll stayed a week and loved every moment. It was one of the few completely pleasant aspects of his involvement with the Dionnes. In January 1937, he wrote to his friend W. L. Clark of the *Windsor Star*: "My flying visit to Hollywood has had a bad effect on me, in that I continually want to go back there for another week."[26]

Sedgwick did an outstanding job of looking after the interests of the children. Croll was able to announce to the legislature that the financial arrangements for the children would yield $880,000 by 1938. He insisted that Dafoe should also be allowed to make some money out of the quints' fame because of his important role. Dafoe, of course, was becoming famous in his own right. In fact, there was speculation that he would be nominated for the Nobel Prize because of his singular contribution to medicine!

At some stage, Croll and Dafoe had a falling-out over Dafoe's demand that the guardianship of the quintuplets be vested solely in himself, something to which Croll could not agree. Finally, tiring of the argument and finding the responsibility of looking after the children's affairs ultimately unrewarding, Croll resigned as guardian on 24 February 1937.[27] As he pointed out to the legislature, his guardianship in 1935 had been necessary to protect the children from both danger to their health and reckless exploitation. He continued:

> It won't be long before they come to the realization that they are unique and the subject of a world-wide publicity campaign. For their own good, we have to do what we can to offset this. They have health; they have money; what they need now most of all is a normal domestic life; association with their brothers and sisters, the love and the discipline which their parents alone can completely provide. There is no substitute for a mother.[28]

For all his trouble, Croll received a long, vituperative letter from Oliva and Elzire Dionne.[29] There were five typewritten pages of abuse, focussing primarily on Croll's alleged short comings as a guardian. Its tone can be judged from the following:

> It is our claim that the present well-being of our separated children is not due to your guardianship nor the ministrations of their physician. God should be given some credit for their

survival, despite the cruel and inconsiderate exploitation which you very ably furthered.

The odd feature of this letter is that it is written in excellent and idiomatic English, something quite beyond the competence of the Dionnes. Oliva Dionne had issued an earlier "Open Letter" to the Pope claiming his children were being held hostage by a Russian communist Jew: that is, David Croll!

There was an ugly occasion when Croll, as minister of public welfare, became caught in a crossfire between the Ontario government and the United Church of Canada. The episode began innocently when Milton Arthur Sorsoleil, the deputy minister of public welfare, made a speech on 20 November 1934 to the presbytery of Toronto Centre of the United Church of Canada. Sorsoleil addressed a luncheon meeting on the subject of church leadership and suggested that adults had set a bad example for children by smoking. According to one witness, the Reverend Garnet W. Lynd, chairman of the presbytery, "he spoke with pathos in his voice and with an occasional tear in his eye, and made a stirring appeal to the Christian men and women present to save the boys and girls."[30]

Sorsoleil's comments about the evils of smoking applied to children in schools run by the Department of Public Welfare for the benefit of the unruly and the incorrigible. The craving for cigarette butts would lead them to criminal activity of an unspeakable nature. Sorsoleil also mentioned that contraceptives had sometimes been offered for sale outside of high schools but did not suggest that this was a common occurrence. The Reverend Mr. Lynd reported that Sorsoleil "even went out of his way in his speech to pay a glowing tribute to his chief, Mr. Croll, as well as to defend, at least in a measure, the Government liquor policy." (Exception was taken to this tribute by some members of the audience, and the vote of thanks was not quite unanimous.) It must have been a slow day for news because a reporter who was present undertook to embellish the speech. The next day the Toronto *Mail and Empire* converted Sorsoleil's statements into an exposé of the moral depravity of schoolchildren in Ontario. According to the press report, immorality was rampant in the schools, condoms were being widely sold at the doors of high schools, and children were collecting cigarette butts from the gutter on their way to church and back. The paper quoted Sorsoleil as saying that about 2,500 illegitimate births were reported to his office every year. His aim in reporting these "terrible conditions" was to challenge the church to devise some remedy. Sorsoleil later explained that he had been misinterpreted and had no intention of disparaging the morals of ordinary schoolchildren. The explanation came too late, and the Hepburn government as well as a number of educational authorities claimed that the charges were grossly exaggerated. In particular, Dr. L. J. Simpson, the minister of education, was reported to be very upset about the remarks of the deputy minister.[31] Croll was very cool about the situation, and all he would say at first was that Sorsoleil was expressing his own personal point of view.

The next step in the drama was that Hepburn, presumably with the support of his cabinet, suspended Sorsoleil. At this point Croll had to make some comment, and he observed, "The nature and gravity of the charges made by a responsible official of the government are such that I feel Mr. Sorsoleil ought to have full opportunity to prove them or demonstrate that he was misquoted."[32] One of the players was a loud-mouthed clergyman, Dr. George A. Little, editor of Sunday school publications for the United Church of Canada. He inserted himself with the rude observation: "just let a Border City Russian Jew dismiss a lifelong Christian worker like Mr.

Sorsoleil for trying to reduce the number of children born out of wedlock in Ontario, and there will come a province wide demand that the Minister of Welfare follow his deputy."[33] By this time, the story was commanding banner headlines in the *Mail and Empire*. Little's slur gave Hepburn precisely the opening he needed, and he was able to hold Little's feet to the fire for his foolish comment. In the midst of these exchanges, Croll was discreet enough to head back to Windsor, out of the line of fire. He was stopped en route by the Ontario Provincial Police and told that the reporters were eager to talk to him, but he would have none of it. Later, according to the press, "Hon. Mr. Croll, at his Windsor home, refused absolutely to be drawn into the controversy."[34]

The United Church was embarrassed by Little's comments, and finally Richard Roberts, the moderator, issued a press release apologizing on behalf of the church for the derogatory remarks about Croll. Roberts said, in part:

> I deeply regret the incident and desire to assure Honorable David Croll that I disassociate myself entirely from any sentiment which would seem to cast contempt on those of another race or creed, particularly on any of that faith to which historic Christendom owes so much. In this it is my judgment that I speak the mind of the people of the United Church of Canada.[35]

After this, public interest in the issue diminished, the honour of the schoolchildren of Ontario remained untarnished, Sorsoleil was reinstated, and the hawkers of contraceptives, if indeed they existed, continued to ply their trade outside the high-school gates. The unfortunate churchgoing children under the care of the Department of Public Welfare, who could not raise a dime for a package of cigarettes, presumably continued to snipe butts in the gutters in Ontario.

While these events were going on, Croll had his hands full with his expanding ministerial responsibilities. The financial position of many municipalities in Ontario continued to deteriorate, and by the mid-1930s some systematic approach to their problems was needed. Accordingly, on 8 August 1934, a new Department of Municipal Affairs was created with Croll as minister.[36] He also retained his portfolio as minister of public welfare. His goal was to impose some order on chaotic municipal finances and to slow the increasing number of defaults on pecuniary obligations without resorting to the autocratic boards of supervisors introduced by the Henry government. By 1935, municipalities were prohibited from any financial undertaking requiring the issue of debentures without the approval of the Ontario Municipal Board. Croll then tightened the screws by amending the Municipal Act to revoke the power of municipalities to levy income taxes.[37]

Because his new ministerial duties involved questions of municipal taxes, Croll could not remain aloof from the imbroglio that developed over separate schools. He had seen some aspects of this issue in Windsor and had concluded that the maintenance of separate schools was essential. Should they close down for lack of funds, there would be an intolerable burden on the nonsectarian school system. Croll also believed that Roman Catholics should be entitled to educate their children in a religious milieu appropriate to their faith.

The very question of Roman Catholic separate schools, however, traditionally brought out some of the worst instincts of the people of Ontario, particularly in the small town and rural areas. The polemics of the Grand Orange Lodge of British America were matched by its Catholic counterpart, and on various occasions the legal quarrels were elevated to the highest courts. Statutory authority for Roman Catholic separate schools predated Confederation and was guaranteed by Section 93(1) of the British North America Act, which prohibited any law that would "prejudicially affect" the rights or privileges of separate schools as these existed at the time of union in 1867. The effect of this guarantee was to preserve separate schools up to the education level of the common or elementary schools. Provincial educational grants had extended separate schools to what is now grade 10, but Roman Catholic efforts to have financial support extended to the senior grades were blocked by a 1928 decision of the Judicial Committee of the Privy Council. Individual Roman Catholics had the right to earmark part of their property taxes for the support of their schools, but the rapid decline in property tax yields after the onset of the depression impaired their ability to carry on. A new source of revenue was badly needed, and the Catholic Taxpayers' Association, under the energetic, if erratic, direction of Martin J. Quinn, began a campaign for a share of corporation and public utility taxes.

On 3 April 1936, Hepburn introduced his new school bill, which provided that corporations would be obliged to divide their school taxes in proportion to the creed of their shareholders. If the corporations could not sort out the beliefs of their shareholders, the ratio of Protestants to Catholics in relevant municipalities would be used to apportion their taxes. No mention was made of public utility taxes. After much contention, the bill was passed on 9 April 1936, and whereas only three Liberals voted against it, there were many in caucus who were unhappy with it. Even within the cabinet there was strong opposition, and Hepburn had to take a firm stand. At one point he said of the legislation, "It's sound and right and fair."[38] This was also Croll's view.

During the campaign for a by-election in East Hastings in December 1936, it became clear just how thoroughly unpopular the legislation was with Ontario's Protestant majority. When the controversy over the funding on Ontario separate schools resurfaced nearly fifty years later and again became a contentious front page issue, the press naturally called on Croll for comments. He recalled that in 1936, the opposition had been based on religious bigotry. For example, there had been a whispering campaign that Casa Loma in Toronto was to become the Pope's Canadian residence and the King's Crown on highway signs was to be replaced by the sign of the Cross. Some of the political meetings were interrupted by organized violence and uncontrolled heckling. He also recalled Hepburn's chagrin at the Liberal defeat in the by-election in East Hastings and his forced retreat on the offending school legislation. The vote in the Ontario legislature on its repeal was 80-0.

Because of his responsibility as minister of municipal affairs, Croll also became involved in a bitter controversy concerning the amalgamation of the Border Cities. The Border Cities consisted of the city of Windsor, the city of East Windsor (once known as Ford City), the town of Sandwich and the town of Walkerville. The estimated population of these places in 1934 was Windsor—63,010; East Windsor—14,954; Sandwich—10,922; Walkerville—9,751.[39] The combined population had dropped more than 8,000 since 1930. The municipalities were contiguous, and there had been agitation for their amalgamation for many years, especially in the 1920s. The *Border Cities Star* had been pressing for union since 1918. The basic objection arose out of the fact that major industrial plants such as Hiram Walker and Sons Limited were in Walkerville, providing Walkerville with a very satisfactory property tax base. The ratepayers of Walkerville were hostile to any amalgamation proposal that would impair their favoured status. The mayor of Walkerville, Russell A. Farrow, in a statement to the Walkerville Town Council on 7 January 1935 foresaw some "shameful" efforts to damage what he had earlier referred to as "our beloved town." He did assure the neighbouring municipalities of Walkerville's interest in the "splendid struggle they have been making to bring some order out of the chaos into which their civic finances have fallen." He then went on to plead for the status quo:

> This, then, brings up the important thought in all our minds, namely, the maintaining of our present form of government, our name and allegiance to tradition. In this regard, it is unnecessary to remind you that certain interests, for no good reason whatsoever, would plunge us into default with our neighbours, and thus remove the last vestige of financial stability within these communities. To be more specific, I would say that the action appears to be one of cold calculation to satisfy the whim of our Member in the Ontario Legislature and in (or out of) turn satiate the ego of a great newspaper.[40]

He then claimed that the Bank of Montreal had refused Walkerville a loan of $100,000 as a result of the intervention of Queen's Park. Farrow spoke of the citizens' mandate "to fight unconditional surrender of rights to the last ditch."

There were streams of delegations to Queen's Park for and against amalgamation, and the powers in Toronto were tired of the whole issue. The controversy intensified during the depression, when property tax receipts plummeted in the region and at the same time relief costs soared. A referendum on amalgamation had been held in the Border Cities in December 1934, and the dichotomy was apparent. The partial results were:

	For	Against
Windsor and East Windsor	12,999	3,152
Walkerville	641	2,553[41]

Croll was firmly convinced of the need for action and accordingly introduced legislation in the Ontario House to amalgamate the Border Cities. The bill provided for the creation of a special finance commission to be appointed initially by the lieutenant governor in council, but later the Commission was to include two appointed members and one person elected by the property owners. One of the members was to represent the interests of the creditors. In speaking on the bill before the legislature, Croll emphasized that it was essential to reduce the debts owed by the municipalities and to alleviate the burden of interest costs. The bill was passed on 17 April 1935.

Croll had the support of Hepburn as well as local members A. H. C. Trottier of Essex North, Lambert P. Wigle of Essex South and James Howard Clark of Windsor-Sandwich. Nevertheless, Croll received the lion's share of the praise (and the calumny). In a signed statement in the *Border Cities Star*, W. F. Herman was almost rhapsodic:

> The victory belongs to Dave Croll. . . . He was the General and the Army rolled into one. . . . When Mr. Croll launched his amalgamation proposal he well knew what lay ahead of him. Does any person believe for one moment that he failed to sense the torrent of abuse for which he was headed, to know that his path would be as thorny as possible? If there be any who believe otherwise, then please disillusion yourself at once. Dave knew all the difficulties and was sure his opponents would see that he was beset with every one of them.
>
> But here's where Mr. Croll differs with a lot of others who want to enjoy public life. He believes public office is a trust; that he must be faithful to that trust. He saw the necessity for amalgamation; he believed this community's progress was being retarded because of its incohesiveness; that the cost of civic administration was too high. Seeing these things and having faith in the soundness of the proposition, a subject close to the heart of so many over a long period—he went ahead and did his duty.[42]

The short title of the act was the City of Windsor (Amalgamation) Act 1935. It was to go into effect on 1 July 1935, an occasion that was celebrated by many but not by all. In Walkerville, a sign was erected depicting a tombstone that said, "Walkerville. Born 1857. Crucified 1935."[43]

The financial position of the border Cities was poor, although Walkerville was in much better shape than the others. The blend of industrial and residential assessments in Walkerville was favourable, but the management of civic affairs was not completely satisfactory. For one thing, the town had issued debentures yielding rates of return that were generous compared with the usual municipal rates in Ontario. The debentures were snapped up by some privileged insiders, however, and were not available to the general investor. One civic official became entangled in a conflict of interest and was forced to resign. Some of the weeping and wailing in Walkerville may not have been entirely for sentimental reasons.

The Ontario government had appointed the Royal Commission on Amalgamation to examine the situation. The chairman was Judge J. J. Coughlin. In its submission to the commission, Walkerville objected to bearing part of the burden of surrounding municipalities, "who have by a foolish economic policy created debts which they cannot repay. . . ."[44] From the lengthy submission, it was obvious that Walkerville looked on forced amalgamation as a catastrophe.

The council's submission was supplemented by briefs from various industries. Hiram Walker and Sons Limited echoed many of the concerns of the town council and noted that the company would incur substantial additional cost. For example, "Dies, labels, prints and stationery involved in the change-over form substantial items in this expense."[45] Hiram Walker did not capitulate easily. Fifty years after amalgamation, its famous "Canadian Club" whiskey showed on the label that it was made in "Walkerville, Ontario, Canada."

Parke, Davis and Company foresaw a similar printing problem.

Ultimately, the commission was to agree unanimously that amalgamation offered the only practical solution to the pressing problems of public finance. The commission did not report until 1 May 1935, by which time the deed was done. Its recommendations provided a reasonable and factual analysis of the problem of amalgamation and made many useful proposals concerning the operation of common services under the new regime.

Sponsoring the amalgamation bill was a courageous political act, since Walkerville was in Croll's riding. However, he indicated to the voters that they would have their innings at the next election. He did not believe that he was permanently hurt by his action, but in fact some of the Walkerville voters never forgave him. The feelings in Walkerville were so strong that a faction undertook to upset the action of the government in the courts. The litigation finally ended up in the hands of the Judicial Committee of the Privy Council, and in 1939 a decision throwing out the appeal of the dissident group was handed down.

In his position as a powerful cabinet minister, Croll was responsible for many patronage appointments. In the 1930s, the rewarding of political friends was looked on with considerable public tolerance and understanding. However, Croll was faced with a special difficulty; he felt he had to be circumspect in the appointment of Jews so as not to fuel existing anti-Semitic attitudes. In consequence, he was far from open-handed, causing disappointment and even animosity among associates with great expectations. Croll was content to use his influence in subtler ways.

FOUR

Marching with the Workers

CROLL OFTEN SEEMED TO BE THE TROUBLE-SHOOTER FOR Hepburn and the government. His handling of the Dionne quintuplets' affairs is a prime example. He was no hatchet man, but on one occasion the premier asked Croll to caution a prominent Liberal politician who had been attempting to exact some toll from the distillers in return for listings by the Liquor Control Board of Ontario. Hepburn said that if the politician did not stop, he would be read out of the party. Croll was also called on to protect Hepburn from any scandal arising out of Hepburn's drinking and partying.

In the latter half of May 1935, Hepburn summoned Croll to his office and told him without fanfare that in addition to his other two portfolios, he was to replace Arthur Roebuck as minister of labour.[1] He was therefore to be responsible for the administration of the Industrial Standards Act, the Hepburn government's major initiative in labour legislation. Its main purpose was to establish legally enforceable codes in specified industries governing such things as hours of work, wages and conditions of work. It was legislation that owed much to the United States National Industrial Recovery Act of 16 June 1933, under which Congress suspended antitrust laws for two years and provided for the introduction of industrial codes to shorten hours, raise wages and inhibit unfair business practices. The Ontario legislation, introduced by Arthur Roebuck on 22 March and given Royal Assent on 18 April 1935, provided that groups of employers and employees could negotiate agreements about wages, hours and conditions of work, and that once a certain percentage of a particular industry was covered by such agreement, its terms would become mandatory for the entire industry.

In a report to the legislature in 1936, Croll announced that in the previous fourteen months, forty wage agreements had been negotiated covering roughly sixty thousand workers.[2] In its first two years, the Industrial Standards Act became applicable to such diverse groups as carpenters, plumbers, bakers, furniture workers, electricians, plasterers and painters. One of the primary aims of this legislation was to squeeze out those industries whose economic survival depended on paying their employees starvation wages. In a speech in the legislature on 1 October 1937, Croll became quite dramatic:

> The Tories must have known that there were sweatshops within a mile of the parliament buildings, where scores of women with pinched white faces plied their needles with aching fingers, hour after weary hour, for a few cents.[3]

He had probably been reading that vade-mecum for Liberals, *Industry and Humanity*.[4]

An Ontario minimum wage law for women (and learners) had been in effect since 1920, but there was a loophole to exempt beginners and part-time workers comprising up to one fifth of the workforce in each plant. An inspection system was supposed to ensure that piece rates in the garment industry were high enough to yield acceptable hourly earnings. By the beginning of 1930, however, conditions had deteriorated and sweatshops were common in Toronto. The 1934 Select Committee of the House of Commons—later the Royal Commission—on Price Spreads under the Hon. H. H. Stevens had produced some startling testimony about wages and conditions of work in the needle trades, and these were widely publicized. Partly because of these revelations, the protection of female workers from economic exploitation became something of a cause célèbre for politicians, the press and the public.

In the dying days of the federal Conservative government, the question of minimum wage legislation to cover male workers came into prominence as well, with Bennett's so-called New Deal. In January 1937, when the Judicial Committee of the Privy Council threw out the federal minimum wage legislation involved on the grounds that it usurped a provincial responsibility, Ontario responded quickly. On 4 March 1937, Croll introduced an amendment to the Minimum Wage Act to cover male workers, in order "to protect workers from one distressing phase of man's inhumanity to man."[5] The amended act covered all wage earners in "any business, trade, work, undertaking or occupation except farm workers and domestic servants." Croll was enthusiastic:

> I am proud to be able to present to the House this legislation, which for me represents the fulfilment of many years of hope; and to the Government as a whole the fulfilment of a pledge to the people of this Province. To the House it will give the opportunity to confer a greater happiness, a better life, upon 400,000 workers, who today have no shadow of protection as to wages and hours of work.[6]

At about this same time, Croll announced new measures to create an Industrial and Labour Board. The new board would consolidate the scattered operations of the Department of

Labour and would administer the Industrial Standards Act, the Minimum Wage Act and the Apprenticeship Act. The board would consult with employers and employees to ascertain prevailing wages, to establish minimum wages and to set conditions of work necessary to promote the physical, moral and intellectual well-being of employees.

Croll's attitude towards the labour movement had been clearly evident before he entered provincial politics. When a number of strikes broke out in furniture and packing plants in Stratford in September 1933, the attorney general of the day, W. H. Price, in response to demands from the local authorities, dispatched squads of provincial police and a small contingent of soldiers to the scene. Four officers and 56 men from the Royal Canadian Regiment in London arrived armed with rifles and Lewis machine guns. They were later joined by reinforcements from Toronto. This military force totalled some 120 men, but the most startling aspect of their expedition was the arrival of 4 Carden Lloyd machine gun carriers, sometimes known as "the wicked wasps of war." The *Toronto Daily Star* described them as "baby armoured military tanks." Two of them broke down between London and Stratford, however, and the *Border Cities Star* reported that one driver was overcome by exhaust fumes and a gunner similarly incapacitated. Perhaps more hazardous to their crews than to any real or imagined enemy, somehow the carriers were manoeuvred into a position of safety in the Stratford armouries, where they remained in a high state of readiness. The whole episode might have occurred in an opera buffa, except that some of the Henry's government's actions were more lunatic than comic.

The popular outrage over this military presence found expression in statements by the Furniture Makers' Union in Stratford, the Canadian Brotherhood of Railway Employees, the International Machinists' Union and others. As mayor of Windsor, Croll added his voice to the chorus with a declaration that the dispatch of troops and tanks to cow the Stratford workers was "an insult and an outrage." He said:

> The Stratford strikers must succeed. They are merely asking for decent living conditions. They are orderly citizens attempting to make up for the shortcomings of the government in organizing for their own protection when, as a matter of fact, they should have had that protection by legislation. Collective bargaining is a fundamental right of all working people. . . . The rights of the mass of the workers are a great deal more important than the rights of a few industrialists.[7]

Croll's wise words, of course, were lost on many Canadian businessmen, who were far from immune when John L. Lewis and the Congress of Industrial Organizations (CIO) began to send shudders through the board rooms of North America in 1935. The concept of industrial unionism was bad enough, but Lewis, with his scowling face and fierce rhetoric, was looked upon by his adversaries as the very incarnation of evil. The CIO, which Lewis and others had formed to organize mass production workers by industry rather than craft, introduced the sit-down strike at the Goodyear Tire and Rubber Company in Akron, Ohio, early in 1936. As a result, the United Rubber Workers, one of the CIO unions, won recognition. Smaller-scale strikes by the United Automobile Workers of America (UAW), another CIO union, occurred at the Kelsey Hayes Wheel Company and Bohn Aluminum in Detroit in the latter half of 1936. The major drive of the UAW was against General Motors. The strike against General Motors actually started in Atlanta, Georgia, but soon spread to Flint, Michigan, the centre of the company's manufacturing operations at that time. In January and February 1937, 100,000 workers went on strike in seventeen plants. Although there was little evidence of sabotage, violence was widespread, par-

63

ticularly in Flint, where the police tried to dislodge the sit-down strikers. Frank Murphy, the governor of Michigan, a liberal and compassionate man, called out the National Guard, not to evict the strikers but to preserve law and order. Murphy, who had been mayor of Detroit from 1930 to 1933, and David Croll were warm friends.[8]

Naturally enough, the CIO also had plans for the miners in northern Ontario, the automobile workers in Windsor and Oshawa and the rubber workers in Kitchener. By early March 1937, sit-down strikes had occurred in Sarnia and Kitchener. Strikes had taken place as well at the Coulter Manufacturing Company in Oshawa, which supplied parts to General Motors of Canada, a wholly owned subsidiary of its American parent.

Despite the historic friendliness of Canada and the United States, many Canadians viewed the UAW as an alien agency. Home-grown union agitators were bad enough, but foreign or-ganizers were considered positively menacing. To some, there seemed a pattern in Canadian labour disputes, such as the Winnipeg strike of 1919, in which outside agitators were in-variably responsible for such trouble as developed. Sometimes it was alleged that these organizers were being *paid*, making them even more suspect. Obviously, union people were at the very least radicals and most likely communists!

Prime Minister Mackenzie King's reaction to the prospect of a UAW organization drive in Ontario was predictable in view of his long experience in industrial relations. It was for-eign to his outlook and background to seek to block the incur-sion of the CIO into Canada, but he was distressed by both the Congress's rhetoric and its tactics and he made it clear that there must be respect for Canadian law. In reply to a planted question in the House of Commons, Ernest Lapointe, the minister of justice, stated firmly that sit-down strikes were il-legal and intolerable.[9]

In Ontario, several other, more immediate anti-CIO influences were at work. One of these was the rural background of the premier. Hepburn was a farmer and was sensitive to the traditional animosity of farmers to labour unions. A widely held view in the countryside was that the labour unions and the big corporations were in league to drive up the prices of the manufactures essential to the operation of the farm and the farm household. Many farmers had the simplistic but firm conviction that increases in urban wages meant higher prices for their binders, ploughs and overalls. To them, the spread of the new, militant labour organization was a menace. They were carefully watching Hepburn, who in turn was keenly aware of the importance of his rural vote.

Hepburn also had intimate connections with a number of Toronto's rich but not quite respectable Bay Street investors and promoters, a coterie of parvenus who were largely an ill-educated and hard-drinking lot. This group included the likes of George McCullagh, editor and publisher of the Toronto *Globe and Mail*, "Sell 'em" Ben Smith, Sir James Dunn, who had assembled Algoma Steel, J. R. Timmins and J. P. Bickell, who were heavily involved in mining in northern Ontario. These men and others of their ilk were appalled at the prospect of industrial unionism's penetrating the timber, pulp and paper, and mining industries. George McCullagh was this group's most articulate spokesman. It was after all W. H. Wright's mining money that had financed the purchase and merger of the Liberal *Globe* and the Conservative *Mail and Empire* on 24 November 1936. McCullagh, who had Hepburn's ear, allegedly told H. A. Bruce, Ontario's lieutenant governor, that "he was out to move Roebuck, Croll and Heenan from the [provincial] Cabinet."[10] Presumably, he wanted to remove Croll and Roebuck because neither had made secret his labour sympathies.

The *Globe and Mail*, not yet even aspiring to be Canada's national newspaper, ran a series of lead and front page editorials throughout March 1937 attacking the CIO and arguing that labour agitators from the United States should be deported and that the federal government should ban future entry of "this dangerous class of foreigners."[11] Hepburn obviously agreed. On 8 March 1937, he was quoted as saying:

> We are not going to tolerate them and I point that out to these people now in this country—professional agitators from the United States—to agitate and foment unrest in our industrial areas. And for the benefit of our own workers, let me add that these of whom I complain are paid officials and obtain their salaries from fees levied against the very workmen whom they are supposed to protect.[12]

Hepburn's minister of public welfare, municipal affairs and labour, however, did not share Hepburn's views. When on 31 March, the local Oshawa UAW representative, Charles H. Millard, approached Harry J. Carmichael, vice president and general manager of General Motors of Canada, with his union's proposals and was rebuffed, Louis Fine, the chief conciliator of the Ontario Department of Labour, offered Croll's services as a mediator. The workers and a company spokesman agreed to this offer, and on the morning of 2 April, there was a meeting in Croll's office at Queen's Park. Croll assured the gathering that relief would be available to the workers if it came to a strike. This was an important concession, since the fledgling Oshawa union had few financial resources and its United States parent had its own concerns, including a major strike against Chrysler in Detroit. Initially, Hepburn did not interfere with Croll's attempts at mediation, perhaps because Croll was able to announce after a further meeting on 2 April that he was "hopeful negotiations will result in a peaceful settlement."[13] And with everything seemingly under control, Croll and Hepburn set off for their respective postlegislative session holidays, Croll to White Sulphur Springs, West Virginia, and Hepburn to Florida. Meanwhile, talks continued between the UAW and General Motors of Canada, and on 7 April Louis Fine stated on behalf of Croll that "considerable progress had been made."[14] On the morning of 8 April, however, the negotiations foundered.

The company's explanation was muted. Referring to the union workers, the plant manager, J. B. Highfield said in a formal statement, "It seems clear that recognition of international jurisdiction is their chief objective. It is a question if such recognition is desirable from the standpoint of Canadian labour and Canadian industry."[15] It must have become clear to the workers that the company was going to stand firm on the question of recognition and that a strike was the only alternative to capitulation.

Hepburn, who had flown back to Toronto on 7 April at the urging of his mining cronies, immediately asked Ottawa to send a contingent of police to deal with anticipated violence in Oshawa.[16] Provincial liquor commissioner E. G. Odette ordered all liquor stores, brewers' warehouse stores and beverage rooms in Oshawa closed indefinitely to minimize disorder. Hepburn stated that no relief would be paid to the strikers by the province. He also banned, through the office of the provincial censor, the showing in Ontario motion picture theatres of newsreels of the strike. And he denounced all those who questioned his actions as CIO sympathizers![17]

Hepburn did everything he could to alarm the public about the anticipated violence in Oshawa. And despite the peaceful demeanour of the strikers, he again appealed to Ottawa for reinforcements. Mackenzie King's diary entry for 13 April reveals his thoughts on Hepburn:

In this he has gone out of his way to raise a great issue in this Country, the frightful possibility of which no one can foresee.

The truth of the matter is that he is in the hands of McCullagh of the Globe, and the Globe and McCullagh in the hands of financial mining interests that want to crush the C.I.O. and their organization in Canada. The situation as he has brought it into being has all the elements that are to be found in the present appalling situation in Spain. Hepburn has become a Fascist leader and has sought to have labour in its struggle against organized capital put into the position of being under Communist direction and control. Action of this kind is little short of criminal.[18]

The obsession of the mining barons with the spectre of the CIO was made clear in a statement of J. P. Bickell, president of McIntyre Porcupine Gold Mines, and J. R. Timmins, president of Hollinger Consolidated Mines, that they would shut down their operations before submitting to CIO domination.[19] Bickell, Timmins and the rest of their group also claimed that Croll had helped the CIO get a foothold in Ontario, apparently not realizing or caring that the CIO already had more than a couple of dozen provincial unions in its ranks before the Oshawa strike, and that no individual minister of labour could have much influence on the course of industrial unionism in Canada. They were able nevertheless to convince Hepburn that Croll had outlived his political usefulness.

On 14 April, Hepburn invited at least one newspaperman[20] into his office, summoned his secretary, Roy Elmhirst, and dictated a letter to be sent separately to Croll and Roebuck:

My dear colleague:

It is with deep regret that I find myself in a position where it is necessary to ask for your resignation as a member of the present Administration, since it is clear to me and all concerned that you are not in accord with the policy of the Government in fighting against the inroads of the Lewis organization and communism in general.

To my way of thinking Ontario faces one of the greatest economic crises in its history and for that reason there must be solidarity and unanimity within our ranks.

Needless to say the decision I have arrived at is one that is causing me both grief and unhappiness but I am determined to carry out that policy which I believe to be in the best interests of the people I was elected to serve.

I deeply appreciate your loyalty up to this point and shall always remember our close and intimate associations both in politics and in a social way and I am unhappy indeed that we have arrived at a parting of the ways on a matter of policy.

There is nothing personal in this matter and I hope that in future I shall always enjoy your friendship as I have in the past.[21]

Both Croll and Roebuck submitted their resignations almost immediately. Croll's letter was remarkable, not only for its content but also for its high literary quality. His reply was clearly not produced on the spur of the moment and must have taken nearly all day to prepare.

Dear Mitch:

In compliance with your written request, I herewith submit to you my resignation as Minister of Public Welfare, Municipal Affairs and Labour for the Province of Ontario.

My regret is that you have made no effort personally to obtain a statement of my views. On Saturday I flew back to Toronto and notified you at one o'clock that my services were available at any time thereafter. I did not hear from you again until this morning, when your letter reached me. Had you so approached me, you would have learned directly that there was only one course which I can conscientiously take, a course which has been my road from the very beginning of my career; that of my own ideals as a Reform Liberal. You knew that those were my ideals when you honored me with an invitation to accept a portfolio; it happens that I have clung to them through these three years and that, now the test is come, I am guided by this higher loyalty.

For instance, I have never swerved from a conviction that the working people have a right to form their associations for the purpose of collective bargaining; that they have the privilege of joining the lawful union of their own choice; that if they, in their wisdom and in their knowledge of the conditions under which they work, consider that they should make the final resort to a strike, then that too is their right; and, having struck, that they shall not be molested if they picket peacefully and within the law. These I have considered are the rights which our law ensures to them and which liberalism throughout the years has upheld.

I have never considered it my duty as Minister of Public Welfare to refuse relief to strikers and so have my Department become the greatest strike-breaker of all. As I have seen it, my responsibility has not been to judge whether the strike is right or wrong; my function has been that of mediator and conciliator, my duty to effect amicable settlement and so restore production in the industry. Thousands of working men and women in the Province of Ontario have come to look to me as their protector and their champion. I feel that I cannot now fail them. If the impression gets abroad that the Government is anti-labour, anti-worker or anti-union, all the very splendid social legislation produced by this Government will become of no value—an industrial peace which I have tried so hard and, until last week, successfully, to establish, will vanish from our Province.

I think I may say without boasting that those policies have earned the respect of both employers and employees in this Province. Certainly when I leave—as I must in the face of your pronouncement and my convictions—I shall have the certain knowledge that no word of valid criticism ever has been uttered against the administration of the difficult departments entrusted to my care. I gave you my unswerving loyalty in return for yours.

So much for my general principles. You will see that they were offended in your policy toward the strike at the General Motors plant in Oshawa. You quarrelled with the right of these workers to join the union of their choice. That it was a union sponsored by the Committee for Industrial Organization was incidental to the fact that these thirty-seven hundred men and women had decided that they wished to exercise their liberty to affiliate with that organization. You based your attack upon a conviction that the C.I.O. should not be permitted to invade Canada, when you must have known that agreements had already been signed by the C.I.O. with the Coulter Manufacturing Company of Oshawa and the Goodrich Tire Company of Kitchener. Indeed, there are today and have been for many months, some ten thousand workers in the Province of Ontario who are members of unions affiliated with the C.I.O.—and most of these ten thousand enjoy the protection afforded by our own Industrial Standards Act. Certainly I had never heard, until you made it, any suggestion of an alliance between the Lewis Unions and the Communists. You must be aware of my consistent opposition to Communism or any other form of dictatorship.

These thirty-seven hundred people in Oshawa are decent, law-abiding and hard-working citizens of Ontario. They believe that they have so great a grievance against their employers that they are justified in using their final effective weapon—the strike. Are they right or wrong in this? I submit to you that it is not for you or for me to sit in judgment upon that point. They are acting within their rights as citizens of Canada and the Empire. Should, as you suggested, "the whole force of the Provincial Government be thrown behind General Motors?" In my opinion, they can well look after themselves.

And I would impress upon you further, that they employed the methods of peaceful picketing, that they attempted no violence, nor have done so at any time since they left the factory. As you know, not one arrest has been made for any offence on the part of the strikers. Should the Government then have treated them as criminals, calling in the police of City, Province and Dominion, to combat a violence that never has eventuated?

Understand me: so long as you announced your antagonism to the sit-down strike and your determination to preserve law and order, and combat all subversive forces, I was fully and completely in accord with your views. I think I demonstrated that clearly in my attitude toward revolt and Communism in such instances as the Crowland relief strike, the relief disorders in York and East York Townships, and the recent strike at the Empire Cotton Mills in Welland, where complete order was preserved. Had you confined yourself to these considerations, then never would there have been the necessity for this letter. But to my way of thinking you have gone beyond this, have passed the borders of Liberalism and have entered the perilous realm of I know not what. If the issue were only Communism, you know I would have stayed with you to the end.

From the first I have asked for only two concessions in the matter of the General Motors strike: recognition of the local union, which then could make whatever affiliations it considered best, so long as it was joining a lawful group; and, second, that there be no withholding of relief from the strikers in the event that need arose. When the original difficulties started and when General Motors refused to meet its employees of Local 222, I summoned both sides to my office and obtained the voluntary withdrawal of Mr. Hugh Thompson, the C.I.O. organizer, with whom the company was refusing to treat. I further requested and seemingly received the agreement of General Motors to deal with their employees who were members of Local Union 222. Negotiations were proceeding favourably, indeed peace seemed certain when suddenly General Motors announced a definite refusal to recognize the local union. In withdrawing finally from the scene, I would urge this upon you: that you advise the company to recognize this local. Thereafter it is the local's privilege to affiliate with any lawful group.

I regret that I have been led to the necessity of passing an opinion upon your policy; of taking upon myself responsibility of saying whether it is right or wrong. I appreciate that this is presumption on my part; I had intended merely to say that I had disagreed with it. You know my origins; I have always been with, and one of, the workers, and I have neither the desire nor the ability to swing at this late date to the other side.

In my official capacity I have travelled the middle of the road, but now that you have put the extreme alternative to me, my place is marching with the workers rather than riding with General Motors. At this late date I cannot oppose unionism and the workers and labour as a whole.

Therefore, and regretfully, I tender to you my resignation as Minister of Public Welfare, Labour and Municipal Affairs. You have received my full support in the past, and will continue to do so on those fiscal and hydro policies which you have handled so ably—no one better than myself knows the conscientious labour you have expended on them to make them a boon to this Province. It is only on matters of social policy that I feel I must follow my own course, remain the Reform Liberal I always have been.

Even in this hour of our differences, at this time when I am disagreeing wholeheartedly with you, I cannot but admire the courage and honesty with which you are following the path which you believe right. It is that same fearlessness and determination which have given to this Province so many wise and generally helpful decisions since you first became Prime Minister.

Finally, I would like to reciprocate your hope that this severance of governmental relations will in no way mar the personal friendship which began between us long before the present Government took office, which has continued uninterruptedly during the years of our administration, and which I firmly hope will survive for all time to come. You will, I trust, realize my sincerity when I refer to the "higher loyalty."

Yours sincerely,
David Croll

Croll's letter was felicitous in all respects, but the one statement that caught the public's attention was "my place is marching with the workers rather than riding with General Motors." A day or so later, the *Toronto Daily Star* quoted the Reverend R. J. Irwin, a Toronto clergyman, as referring to Croll's "splendid aphorism" and predicting that it would live for some time to come. This forecast proved correct, as can be seen from entries in *The Dictionary of Canadian Quotations and Phrases* by Robert M. Hamilton and Dorothy Shields (1982), *Colombo's Canadian Quotations* (1974) and *Colombo's Canadian References* (1976), all of which refer to "marching with the workers."

Not unexpectedly, Toronto's leading Liberal paper came to the defence of the two ex-ministers. In a lead editorial on 15 April 1937, the *Toronto Daily Star* stated categorically:

Mr. Hepburn has denied Labour its fundamental right, has spoken and acted provocatively, and has, as a result, lost the two most outstanding members of his cabinet. These two men have refused to sacrifice their conscientious beliefs and their adherence to the welfare of the workers on the altar of Mr. Hepburn's impetuous, unwise and unfair attacks on the rights of Labour. Time will vindicate Mr. Roebuck and Mr. Croll. They are already vindicated in the minds of those who have seen through Mr. Hepburn's shallow pretence that he is fighting communism, when what he is really fighting is the right of workers to choose whatever union will, in their opinion give them the strongest hope of legitimately improving their position.

On 23 April, a bare nine days after Croll's forced resignation, the Oshawa UAW voted, by a margin of 2,205 to 36, to accept the terms of a new contract negotiated the day before. Most of the bread and butter issues had been resolved satisfactorily, but there was still some question about the recognition of Local 222. General Motors had agreed to enter into a contract with "the local union" of its employees, but specific references to Local 222 of the UAW were left out. For example, C. H. Millard and E. E. Bathe signed for the workers as president and vice-president, respectively, but there was no reference to the organization of which they were officers. Millard said afterwards, "I know and they know and the world knows that the union has been recognized. All this business of trying to avoid saying so in so many words is just child's play."[22]

In addition to Roebuck and Croll, there were two other casualties in the sorry affair. Roger Irwin, Croll's secretary, resigned along with his minister. He afterwards joined the staff of the *Toronto Daily Star*. A day or so after the end of the strike, Paul Leduc, the minister of mines, who had taken over from Roebuck as attorney general, announced a reorganization of his new department. Without public explanation, he fired Joseph Sedgwick, senior solicitor in the department. Initially appointed by the Henry government, he had, of course, been closely associated with both Roebuck and Croll. Sedgwick went into private practice and continued to be an adornment to the bar of Toronto and Canada for the rest of his life.

Whereas the Oshawa strike was a milestone in Croll's career and profoundly affected his personal fortunes, it had much broader implications for Ontario and the country generally. The settlement was a victory for the new industrial unionism. The big issue in labour/management disputes in the mid-1930s was union recognition, and the capitulation of General Motors of Canada was a signal that times were changing. There was a political backlash as well. Hepburn, who clearly wanted to break the strike and the union, became embittered by the federal government's lack of co-operation, which doubtless further contributed to the continuing deterioration in his personal and political relations with Mackenzie King. Without question the strike also improved the fortunes of the Socialist Co-operative Commonwealth Federation (CCF) both federally and provincially and contributed to the long winter of the Ontario Liberal party. For all these reasons, it has been described as "a landmark of Canadian labour history."[23]

FIVE

Full Circle

ALTHOUGH IT MAY NOT HAVE SEEMED SO AT THE TIME, IT was a piece of good fortune for Croll to be cut loose from Hepburn, who was becoming increasingly obsessive and irrational, his youthful charm and panache diminishing along with his physical and mental capacities. Croll, in contrast, emerged from their encounter a hero, his principles intact and his political future assured. After the split, relations between Croll and Hepburn consisted mainly of perfunctory greetings. The old intimacy was finished. They talked about the weather or asked about their respective families but never mentioned the issue that divided them. When Hepburn died prematurely, he was not greatly mourned. Croll was the only one of his former cabinet ministers who showed up at the funeral.

In the summer of 1937, however, Hepburn was still riding high politically. He enjoyed widespread support for trying to repulse the CIO, and the election called for 6 October seemed a golden opportunity to smite the Conservatives once more.

Croll was unanimously nominated as Liberal candidate in Windsor-Walkerville by an enthusiastic crowd of three thousand on 12 August. One of Croll's supporters, Malcolm

Caullay, formerly a member of the Walkerville town council, told the meeting:

> Dave Croll has always stood by the people who stood by him. Their interests have always been his interests; their troubles, his troubles. His record as member of the Hepburn Cabinet speaks for itself. Every move, every act he has taken has been from a heart that has always beat in sympathy with the under-dog.[1]

Croll's political status may have been temporarily obscure because of his break with Hepburn, but throughout his long career, he never wavered in his loyalty to the Liberal party. At one point in this period, he was approached by some leading socialists and asked to switch his allegiance. And although it appeared there was an opportunity for him to lead the CCF in Ontario, he rejected the chance, not on ideological grounds but for practical reasons. His ideas on social policy were not greatly different from those of the CCF, but he felt that he could achieve what he wanted only in the Liberal party. As a man of action, he did not put much faith in rhetoric. He also categorically denied reports that he was forming a third party.

Hepburn was quoted as saying that Croll was the official Liberal candidate in Windsor-Walkerville,[2] but the fact was that he could count on no financial help from the party organization in Ontario. If Croll felt any bitterness towards Hepburn, he concealed it very well. At his nomination meeting, according to the *Windsor Star*, "when he spoke of Premier Hepburn there was no bitterness or rancor in his voice. He spoke highly of the premier, praising his keen mind... and his indomitable courage."[3] Croll was quoted as saying, "For three years I had daily and close contact with the premier. I found him a warm-hearted friend. I found him impetuous but able, very able."[4]

Throughout the campaign, Croll made no effort to dissociate himself from the Hepburn administration but emphasized the fine things that had been accomplished, and did his best to avoid the thorny issue of labour strife. In one of his speeches, he warned his audience that a vote for the Conservatives was unthinkable, saying, "You cannot support this party of reaction: you must march forward with the Liberal party." And "a wolf in sheep's clothing," he claimed, "is nothing compared to a Tory in overalls." At the same time, he said that a vote for the CCF was a vote "gone with the wind." He aligned himself fully with Hepburn government, claiming that in 1934

we found that relief standards had been allowed to drop to starvation levels. Thousands of men, women and children were living in miserable conditions on a pittance from the province. A whole section of the population, ragged and hungry had not been treated as human beings by the Conservative government.

We increased relief standards in 350 municipalities, spent every cent we could spare to raise the living standards of our people and restore their health and self-respect. The Hepburn government never hesitated to put human standards first.

The Hepburn government placed on the statute books more progressive social legislation within the space of three years than the reactionary Tory government of the previous 30 years had ever thought of.[5]

As examples, he cited the extension of mothers' allowances to mothers with only one child and the removal of children from shelters to foster homes. He also spoke of the "Adopt-a-Baby" campaign of 1935. He boasted of the beneficial effects of the Industrial Standards Act. So far as the minimum wage for men was concerned, it was almost as if he were speaking for the government:

> The machinery for enforcing the minimum wage act for men has not yet been put into operation but if the Liberal government is returned to power immediate steps will be taken to bring it into force.[6]

Hepburn was saying the same thing in newspaper advertisements.

Locally, the Conservatives nominated one of their most prestigious members, Dr. R. D. Morand, to oppose Croll. Morand came from an old French-Canadian family in the Windsor area and had been deputy speaker of the House of Commons for a period, as well as minister of soldiers' civil re-establishment and minister of health during Meighen's brief tenure as prime minister in 1926. Morand was backed by the Walkerville *News*, which on 5 October devoted the bulk of a special issue to a scurrilous attack on Croll. It claimed that Croll "amassed a fortune in Toronto" while he was a cabinet minister and that he had lived in "the luxurious Royal York Hotel." In fact, the hotel, which had just opened and was in search of a residential clientele, had been happy to accommodate him at the rate of fifty dollars a month. The paper went on to reveal that Croll, his claim to be a man of genuinely modest means to the contrary, belonged to "an exclusive club which has an entry fee of $500 and annual dues of $1,000." This was also true so far as it went, but the country club in question, which was in Detroit, had waived its fees for Croll. On the Canadian side of the river, Croll would not have been welcome. A banner headline stated, "Croll is Communists'

Candidate," and the accompanying story claimed, quite correctly, that Croll's candidacy had been endorsed by the *Daily Clarion*, the Communist newspaper in Toronto, on 24 September. (Arthur Roebuck's bid for re-election in Toronto Bellwoods was also supported by the *Clarion*.) Croll publicly welcomed the Communist support, saying at an election rally, "I'll take endorsement from any group of people who like the kind of government I give them, because I'm willing to serve all sections of the labouring people."[7]

When the votes were counted, the Liberals had retained their decisive majority.

Party	1934	1937
Liberals	66	63
Conservatives	17	23
Miscellaneous	7	4

Croll, likewise, won handily in Windsor-Walkerville, with only fourteen fewer votes than in 1934. In his column in the *Windsor Star*, W. L. Clark commented:

> The smashing victory of Dave Croll in Windsor-Walkerville was even greater than his supporters had predicted.
>
> *The victory was of special significance because Mr. Croll was made the target for some of the dirtiest mudslinging and rottenest tactics that have ever been witnessed in any political campaign, anywhere.*[8]

The Windsor paper also carried this curious quotation from Hepburn the day after the election, datelined St. Thomas, 7 October:

> "Good old Dave! I knew he'd do it. Oh! that's splendid." That's what Premier Hepburn said last night when the word flashed over the wire that Dave Croll Liberal candidate in

Windsor-Walkerville had been elected by a thumping majority.

Either Hepburn or the reporter must have been in his cups!

When the legislature met in December 1937, it sat for only two days. Croll and Roebuck occupied what is known in the British House of Commons as the cross benches and in the Ontario legislature as bad boys' row. In other words, they were designated independent Liberals. Croll, however, was invited to join the government caucus; Roebuck was not. On 10 March 1938, Croll was selected as chairman of the Private Bills Committee of the legislature, a position of some consequence. He was nominated by Liberal whip Ian Strachan on the recommendation of Hepburn, a move seen as healing in some degree the rift between Croll and the premier.[9]

In constant demand as a speaker before political and other audiences, Croll was able to keep his name and views before the public. For example, on 6 March, speaking to a forum in Hamilton, he denounced the twin menaces of fascism and communism. Bringing his remarks closer to home, he excoriated the Duplessis padlock law in Quebec and Premier William Aberhart's attempt to muzzle the press in Alberta. About the padlock law, which the King government was unwilling to disallow or otherwise challenge as ultra vires, he said:

> Nothing more vicious has ever been conceived in the mind of a person calling himself a Canadian. It has converted Quebec into a stamping ground for the ignorant puppet police who carry out the unexplained and unexplainable laws of a government that has never received a mandate to enact such anti-democratic laws.[10]

The role of a backbencher, however, was not particularly onerous in the prewar period. In 1938, the Ontario legislature met only once, from 23 February to 8 April, and in 1939, from 8 March to 27 April. With time hanging heavy on his hands, Croll was itching to become reinvolved in civic politics. His ministerial duties had precluded his running for re-election as mayor in either 1934 or 1936. Consequently, he decided to enter the municipal lists of a substantially expanded Windsor in the fall of 1938.

The bitterness of the amalgamation controversy was still in the forefront of municipal politics. Thus, when Croll ran for mayor in 1938, he was facing a united and determined Walkerville opposition that rallied to the support of the incumbent Windsor mayor, E. S. Wigle, who was seeking re-election. Wigle had first been elected mayor of Windsor in 1905 and again in 1907. He was elected for his third term in 1936, at the age of seventy-six. An establishment figure, he was a well-known lawyer and the officer commanding the Essex Scottish when Croll first crossed his path around the end of World War I.

The 1938 campaign was rough, much like the provincial election of the year before. One newspaper advertisement read "Vote Wigle and Prevent a Communist Victory."[11] Croll liked and respected Wigle, who had after all been his father's lawyer for many years, and did not believe that Wigle personally condoned the actions of his campaign managers. In fact, Croll thought that the bitterest attacks on him were inspired by the executives from the automobile companies in Windsor and reflected their antiunion bias. The most venomous canard was that Croll had written to his political friends in Ottawa asking them to find him a safe berth should war break out. This act was supposed to provide clear evidence of Croll's cowardice and lack of patriotism. Herb Gray, later to become a cabinet minister under Trudeau, recalled:

My first memory of politics is the bitter mayoralty campaign in the city in 1938 between David Croll and Colonel Wigle. I

84

was seven then, but all the kids took sides in it and who knows what impact that had upon me.[12]

Croll's speeches focussed on his ideas about social welfare and related issues: unemployment insurance, a shorter work week, pensions, national health insurance, the unrestricted right of labour to organize and the humanitarian administration of those measures to assist the needy that are essential to the dignity of the people affected. One might argue that Croll should have been running for the provincial or federal parliament, but this mayoralty race prompted the expression of the philosophic foundation on which he was to build for the rest of his public life. Besides, he had neither the obligation nor the intention of abandoning his seat in the provincial legislature. The outcome of the voting on 5 December 1938 was decisive, if less than a landslide:

David A. Croll	19,798
E. S. Wigle	14,277
Roy C. Haight	990

The *Windsor Star* had some kind words for Croll in an editorial, though by this time his friend W. F. Herman had died:

> A brilliant political general, he organized his forces in the way best calculated to secure victory. His magnetic personality once more caught the public imagination and he added another imposing laurel to the string that started with his first election as mayor of Windsor in 1930.[13]

One of the interesting aspects of the election was the unprecedented involvement of a provincial premier in a municipal election. Reginald Whitaker notes that Croll was elected despite Hepburn's "vigorous personal intervention" by means of an open letter against Croll's campaign platform of home rule for Windsor. The sympathies of both the *Windsor Star* and the premier are evident in a news story that appeared the day after the election:

> Premier Hepburn appeared today to be none too pleased about the election of Dave Croll as mayor of Windsor.
>
> Mr. Hepburn took few pains to disguise his pique. The following message to the Star's Toronto correspondent from the Star's news editor was read to him. "Could you get comments from Premier on Mr. Croll's victory? No thought of rubbing it in. Rather it would be splendid if he said Windsor civic administration will continue to receive fullest co-operation from Queen's Park and that he feels Windsor will go forward under Croll's guidance."
>
> But Mr. Hepburn said this: "All I ask is that Mr. Croll do the things he promised to do; that he reduce the age at which old age pensions may be received and he increase relief allowances; that he persuade the Ontario Government to contribute 50 per cent of the cost of education; that he secure a share of the gasoline tax for municipalities; that he gain a larger proportion of the revenues from the Liquor Control Board of Ontario for municipalities, that he reduce the fare on the S. W. and A. [Sandwich, Windsor & Amherstburg Railway] and that he provide a job for every unemployed man in Windsor.
>
> "I will watch with interest to see if he succeeds," the Premier added unable to conceal the sarcasm in his tone.[14]

Early in January 1939, Croll delivered his inaugural address to the city council, in which he pledged to work for a self-governing city, free of industrial conflict, with better conditions for taxpayers and relief recipients. He emphasized that

the city must be unfettered to manage its own affairs and announced his goals of a five-cent carfare, a higher scale of relief, and rigid economy in the conduct of civic affairs.[15]

The Royal Tour of 1939 was a momentous event for many
Canadians and provided a minor role for Croll and his family.
Not only were King George VI and Queen Elizabeth personally popular, but their visit was the first time a reigning British
monarch had set foot in Canada. The happy prospect was
soured in Windsor when it was revealed that the town was not
included in the planned itinerary.[16] This omission provoked a
loud protest from the citizens and particularly the *Windsor
Star*. The local political figures were besieged with demands
that the oversight be corrected. Croll wired Mackenzie King
asking for reconsideration and descended on the federal Liberal members from the area, including Norman McLarty, the
federal M.P. for Essex West and postmaster general; Paul
Martin, the member from Essex East; and Murray Clark, the
member from Essex South. A delegation from the Windsor
City Council and Paul Martin went to Ottawa to plead their
case before the tour officials.[17] King or the staff arranging the
tour saw the light, and the schedule was juggled to include a
brief stopover in Windsor.

The festive day was 6 June, and thousands of people came
from Ontario and at least ten neighbouring states to welcome
the royal couple. The official reception was in the railway station. Croll was there, in full fig, with his wife and family.
Mackenzie King was very much in evidence. Constance
Croll, then ten and a very pretty girl, presented Queen Elizabeth with an elaborate bouquet. A six-column picture of this
tableau on the front page of the *Windsor Star* showed King
George, Mackenzie King and Sarah Croll looking on.[18] The
elite of Windsor and Essex County, dressed in their best,
gathered in the station to greet the royal couple. Among
those formally received were Croll's friend Mayor Richard

Reading of Detroit and his wife. Henry Ford was invited, but he did not come.

On 31 August 1939 Croll addressed the Ontario Municipal Association, urging heavier reliance on the taxing powers of the provincial and federal governments and less on municipal property taxes. He contended that taxes on land and buildings were far too one sided and had a dampening effect on the building industry. He also argued that it was important for municipal councils to have some measure of control over the expenditures of boards of education, something that might be achieved by having council representatives sit on each school board.[19] On the very next page of the newspaper reporting this meeting, however, the headline read, "Britain Mobilizes Fleet and Orders Censorship." Attention was rapidly moving away from the problems of property taxes and municipal finances.

SIX

A Private War

By the time World War II broke out in September 1939, Croll was a seasoned politician, with an extended network of connections at every level of government. Yet like most other Canadians, he was taken by surprise when Poland was invaded. His immediate reaction was to join the fight.

About two weeks after war was declared, he approached the local army recruiting office. At that time, efforts were being made to bring the Essex Scottish up to wartime standards. The commanding officer, Lt. Col. Arthur S. Pearson, explained that he could not enlist Croll because there were no vacancies within his regiment's complement of officers.

Croll would probably not have been completely welcome anyway. The majority of the Essex Scottish officers would have come from Walkerville, where the bitterness of the amalgamation controversy was very much alive. Croll's name was anathema to them, and his reputation for being a radical in politics was a further obstacle. In the inner circles of Walkerville, being a Jew was no great advantage either. Croll, however, was not to be deflected. He insisted on enlisting as a private soldier. For ten days, he stormed the orderly room until Pearson reluctantly agreed to take him on.

The reasons for Croll's determination were complex. Part of his credo was *Dulce et decorum est pro patria mori*.[1] Perhaps his father's participation in the Russo-Japanese War of 1904 and 1905 influenced him. The threat of fascism and the persecution of the Jews by the Nazis were also powerful motives. The dominant reason was less obvious. In his many dealings with veterans of World War I, he had repeatedly heard that Jewish soldiers were concentrated in the service corps rather than in the fighting troops. In consequence, Croll was determined that he would set a high-profile example as a fighting soldier and, if necessary, a private.

Croll's friend Norman Rogers was now minister of national defence. After Croll enlisted, he discussed his military career with Rogers, who suggested that Croll be seconded, with appropriate rank, to his office in Ottawa. Croll refused, pointing out that Rogers had gone overseas as a private in World War I and he was going to do the same. The crucial fact that Croll neglected was that Rogers was twenty years old in 1914, not thirty-nine.

Croll was fighting a private war in the midst of the larger conflict. However praiseworthy his motives and determination, he underestimated the monolithic character of the army and its tradition of conservatism. Rules and orders were to be obeyed, not circumvented, and he would ultimately suffer the consequences of his presumption at the hands of the military bureaucracy.

Croll was duly sworn in as Pte. David A. Croll on 6 October 1939 with I Battalion, The Essex Scottish Regiment. The regiment spent the early months of the war in Windsor, where it did its preliminary training. This training consisted of weapons instructions, route marches and repetitive drill. In the fall of 1939, it was not an unusual sight to see Croll at city council meetings in his kilted uniform. Shortly after Christmas, the regiment was shipped off to Camp Borden for infantry training before being sent overseas. In Borden, Croll trained as a rifle-man. Although it is difficult to prove, there are indications that Croll's life as a private soldier was made unusually diffi-cult because of his role in civilian life. He was under the thumb of his political enemies, and they did him no favours. In addition, the soldiers Croll trained with were compara-tively young, and he did not readily share their pastimes. His physical condition was excellent, however, and he was not troubled by the rigours of training. He had the body of a twenty-eight-year-old.

On 23 July 1940, Croll embarked for England with his regi-ment. They travelled on the troop transport E53 and were es-corted by HMS *Revenge*. After an uneventful voyage to Gourock in the Firth of Clyde, they entrained for Aldershot, about sixty-five kilometres from London, where they arrived on 3 August. During his first leave in London, Croll was in the gallery of the House of Commons when Winston Chur-chill paid his famous tribute to the Royal Air Force: "Never in the field of human conflict was so much owed by so many to so few."

Early in his stay in England, Croll has honoured at a dinner given for him by the Royal Borough of Windsor. The dinner reflected in part Britain's welcoming of the newly arrived Ca-nadian soldiers during the dark days of 1940 and in part the sentimental ties between the two Windsors. His Worship Mayor David A. Croll was received with pomp and ceremony, and he was somewhat overawed by the assembled brass. There were representatives of the local authorities, including the mayor, Norman Butler, the peerage, the church and the mili-tary gathered to do honour to a Canadian private soldier. It was altogether a grand occasion, but like Cinderella, Croll had to return to harsh reality all too soon.

Some concern developed almost immediately about Croll's employment in England. On 30 August, the general officer commanding the 2nd Division, Maj. Gen. Victor W. Odlum, wrote to the senior officer at Canadian Military Headquarters in London pointing out that Private Croll was a member of the Legislative Assembly in Ontario and had been a provincial cabinet minister. He was also mayor of Windsor and had been granted leave of absence to proceed on active service. Odlum recommended that he be sent to the Canadian Officer Cadet Training Unit at Bordon Camp, Hampshire, in order to qualify for a commission. As a result, on 2 September Croll was admitted to a class that had started on 5 August.

Shortly after Croll's arrival at Borden Camp, Lt. Gen. A. G. L. McNaughton, the commander of the Canadian Corps, inspected the Officer Cadet Training Unit and discovered to his distress that two candidates, one of them being Croll, had been enrolled in the course after it had started. This was contrary to the policy he had laid down. Consequently, the two unfortunates were returned to holding units forthwith. It may appear odd that a corps commander should concern himself with such trivia, but perhaps meticulous attention to detail was a prerequisite for senior command. Canadian Military Headquarters, however, acted with equal dispatch, and by 13 September Croll had been posted to the British Officer Cadet Training Unit at Sandhurst. The Royal Military Academy at Sandhurst had long been famous as a training ground for subalterns in the British army.

Croll's experience at Sandhurst was enjoyable, and despite his colonial status, he found his British classmates and instructors congenial. For one reason, Croll was an excellent squash player and played regularly with the officers, who respected athletic prowess. The level of discipline was high, and the officers were held in awe by the cadets. Because Croll was older than most of the others, he was given a private room, where he devoted himself to assiduous study. He had a fear of failure and was determined that he would give the instructors no cause to fault him. He went to the local pub on Saturday nights to let his fellow cadets know he was alive, but the rest of the time he worked like a staver in his little room.

Croll wrote an account of the routine at Sandhurst, which was published in the Windsor paper early in November 1940. The excerpt from a letter was headed with the usual "Somewhere in England":

At the school here the course is really rough—reveille at 5:30, cup of tea 6:15, parade 6:30–8 and real drill. Breakfast 8–8:30, then parades again and lectures and exercises to one o'clock, lunch one to 2 and then parades again until 4!

Twice a week we have night exercises. Wednesday afternoons free for games, soccer, rugger and field hockey. Lights out at 10:30. Every day we stand to for one hour and we have night duties for passive air defence and fires. Guards and anti-aircraft defence come in regular turns on top of all that.

I just came back from church parade, which is the big event of the week here. We dress in our very best and the crease in our trousers must be the crease that cuts, with shoes that shine and I mean shine.

We are given a minute inspection, even behind the buttons. Then we line up with white bands around our hats and on our epaulets, with a Sam Browne belt and bayonet that shines for miles. We walk to church as one man. Really, Hollywood can learn from this place.

We are led by a high officer who is preceded by two heralds wearing white jackets and followed by officers marching like toy soldiers. All the people in the vicinity come for their Sunday treat. It's an old custom and they all turn out to see us march four blocks. And the marching is really worth seeing.

The grand ladies in furs and jewels come from all around and seem particularly prominent but they are after all just a few. The rest are folks from the village and this is their one treat of the week, if they can forget the Hun. As soon as we hear him the parade is over, but for the second time since I've been here we got through today without a mishap.[2]

Croll completed the course on 20 December 1940. The periodic reports of the company commander were very satisfactory:

COMPANY COMMANDER'S REPORT

1st month	Croll has been a surprise. His age and past position might have made it difficult for him to absorb the subjects taught here. Not at all. He is second in his platoon in both written tests, is very hard-working, most popular in his platoon (and a good influence) and very eager to learn. 13 Oct 40
2nd month	He is still doing excellently in his work here. He is, perhaps, finding it a little difficult to acquire the disciplinarian outlook of the English Army but this is my only comment on his work here so far. 14 Nov 40
3rd month	This cadet has extracted all he could from this course. He has been a valuable asset in the

Company and is liked by everybody. He should
be a most valuable officer. 15 Dec 40

COMMANDING OFFICER'S REMARKS

Category B   A fine achievement in every way.

Croll was commissioned as a lieutenant in the Essex Scottish on 21 December and at the same time was posted to the
No. 1 Infantry Holding Unit as a reinforcement. Then, for
reasons that can only be surmised, Croll was assigned to the
13th War Intelligence Course at Matlock (Witley) for the period 25 January to 22 February 1941. Croll again worked hard
when he was on this course. He was surrounded by experienced and senior British officers, many with the rank of major
and colonel. At times, he found himself in disagreement with
the approach of the military instructors, perhaps because he
was still a civilian at heart. Consequently, his results were
mixed, but his final report was unflattering. After this indoc-
trination, Croll was posted to a unit of the Canadian
Armoured Corps, the 8 Reconnaissance Battalion (14 Canadian Hussars), on 14 March.

In Croll's various postings in England, he was never far
from London. When he had leave, he regularly visited the
House of Commons, where because of his membership in the
Empire Parliamentary Association, he was always assured a
seat for himself and a companion. He was, he recalls, always
slightly embarrassed passing the long queues of senior officers
and other worthies waiting for admission.

Croll did not find his sojourn with the 8 Reconnaissance
Battalion either very demanding or very exciting. There were
assorted training exercises, but there were also long periods of
inactivity. These he filled in by writing a small training man-

ual for dispatch riders. The textual material (twenty-seven pages) is written simply, with some flashes of humour, and stresses the responsibility of riders and the various techniques of safe and efficient travel, mainly on motorcycles. It was combined with an ingenious grouping of the conventional map signs under the letters of the alphabet. For example, under the letter A were shown the signs for aerodromes, antiquities, aqueducts and altitude. The booklet was especially valuable to troops whose mother tongue was not English because it relied heavily on symbols. Surprisingly, in view of the normally superior attitude of the British to colonials, the War Office agreed to publish the booklet, which appeared with the title *Despatch Rider's Primer and Alphabet of Map Reading* (Aldershot, Eng.: Gale & Polden Ltd., 1941). He sent an inscribed copy to MacKenzie King and received a polite acknowledgement from G. P. Vanier. The price was one shilling, and royalties equivalent to about eight hundred dollars accumulated, which Croll recommended be distributed among the welfare funds of the three services.

Croll's various attempts while in England to join a unit with some prospect of action in the field were frustrated by superiors unsympathetic to his requests that the rules governing age be set aside in his instance. In March 1942, clearly not very happy in the service, he was returned to Canada to serve with the Oxford Rifles in Woodstock. Effective 1 April that year, he was promoted to the rank of captain. In the summer of 1942, there was a vacancy for a major in the 30 Reconnaissance Battalion (Essex Scottish), for which Croll was recommended by Brig. D. J. MacDonald, Officer Commanding, Military District No. 1:

In the absence of other qualified officers the name of Captain David Croll of the Oxford Rifles should receive consideration for a vacancy in the rank of major.

This officer, it is understood, served fourteen months with a reconnaissance battalion overseas and also was instrumental in preparing one of the training pamphlets used by reconnaissance units. His services with the Oxford Rifles have been most satisfactory.

Due to his strong personality and leadership of a radical faction in the City of Windsor the desirability of his introduction in senior rank into a Windsor unit, of which he was not formerly a member, appeared to be somewhat questionable. . . .

Giving due consideration to all the foregoing factors, I wish to recommend that Captain Croll be transferred to the 30th Recce Battalion in the rank of major. I would like to add that I have found his bearing and deportment very satisfactory since his return from overseas and that he has been zealous and keen in his duties.

Despite this recommendation, the job was given to someone else and Croll was left to soldier on.

In the fall of 1942, his regiment was moved to Prince George, headquarters of the 8th Division. On 16 March 1943, Croll was promoted to the rank of major and sent to the 9th Senior Officers' Course at the Royal Military College in Kingston. The assessment of Croll at the end of this course, which lasted from 17 April to 19 June 1943, was flattering. He was classed as a good leader, aggressive and convincing. In various other categories, his ratings ranged from "great" to "very good" to "good," and his personality was described as "pleasant and cooperative." The general remarks noted that he was "a sound, determined officer with a good background of knowledge. A very good student." His overall grading was B—above average. On 27 June, he rejoined his regiment, which had been moved to Wainwright, Alberta.

A request from the adjutant general to Canadian Military Headquarters in London concerning an overseas assignment for Croll was turned down on 2 June 1943, on the grounds that Croll was overage. His name was then submitted by Pacific Command for attachment to the Australian and New Zealand Forces for service in the Pacific theatre. When this proposal was considered by the Officers' Survey and Classification Board, his name was again deleted on grounds of age. On 4 September Croll was formally designated second-in-command of the Oxford Rifles.

While Croll was rusticating in Wainright with not even buffaloes for company, the political situation in Ontario was coming to a boil. A provincial election was scheduled for 4 August 1943, and Harry Nixon, who had succeeded to the premiership in April, urged Croll to let his name stand again in his home ground of Windsor-Walkerville. Croll reluctantly agreed, but he could not campaign and in fact did not participate at all in the election. His wife and friends did what they could, but the tide was turning against the Liberals. The results were:

William C. Riggs (PC)	6,711
David A. Croll (L)	4,334
Angus W. MacMillan (CCF)	4,124

This was the only election that Croll ever lost. He was in good company, as Nixon and many other Liberal stalwarts were swept away. The final standings were:

Progressive Conservative	38
CCF	34
Liberals	15
Labour Progressive	2
Independent Labour	1

In the best military tradition, Croll took another course, this time on the construction and maintenance of outhouses.

The next important step in Croll's military career came about in consequence of a highly irregular initiative. On 12 December 1943, he wrote a confidential letter to J. L. Ralston, the minister of national defence, who had been a political friend for many years, to ask for his intervention:

My work here is done. My regiment because of the H. D. [Home Defence] Personnel is not going any place. That has not always been my conviction but it is firmly established in my mind at the present time.

Our troops are now engaged at least on one front, but I who have been in the Army from the start have not seen action, and under the present circumstances am not likely to see action. In that respect I am almost alone of the original officers of the Essex Scottish, a very unhealthy situation.

My position is a very difficult one. I feel utterly humiliated and am having a very difficult time living with myself. I know what this war is about, and I am certainly not doing my share remaining where I am at present.

I know how reluctant you are to deal with such matters, but I ask under the circumstances you stretch a point and give me combat duties.

As a result of the inquiries stemming from Croll's brash appeal, a number of assessments of Croll's aptitude and character were produced, one of them being the unflattering comment on the intelligence course he had taken at Matlock. The long and the short of it was that the Canadian military brass rejected the proposal that Croll be accepted for service in any combat capacity, but recommended that he be exposed to civil affairs training in Kingston. This recommendation was taken seriously, and Croll distinguished himself in the Canadian Civil Affairs Staff Course, which lasted from 8 May until 1 July 1944. He emerged with an A standing, which was reflected in the remarks of the course staff:

> This officer is a legal specialist with an excellent adm background. He has character, judgement and good knowledge. Is unassuming but well liked. Outstanding in ability with well developed qualities of leadership. He has initiative, drive and sound practical ideas.

Croll was transferred from the Oxford Rifles effective 6 May 1944. In effect, he had lost his personal war with the army. He would never fire a shot in anger.

By the late summer of 1944, Croll was on his way back to England as a civil affairs specialist. Shortly after his arrival, he was promoted to the rank of acting lieutenant colonel. On 7 September, he was transferred to 21 Army Group under the command of Field-Marshal Montgomery. A few days later, he embarked for France. Teams from the Allied Military Government pool were given responsibility for displaced persons and ex-prisoners of war, as well as the civilian population in general. One of the crucial problems was to maintain public utilities and other essential services in captured areas. Croll was a member of a pool of officers assigned to different places in France, Holland, Belgium and Germany as the need arose. At one stage he was attached to the First Canadian Army, which was operating in the Netherlands.

Paul Martin, in his autobiography, gives an account of a visit to General Crerar's headquarters early in February 1945, just before the beginning of the battles in the Reichswald and Hochwald forests.[3] He wanted to see something of military government in captured areas, and one of the first people he ran into was Croll, then the military administrator of 's Hertogenbosch, a provincial capital north of Eindhoven. Martin, M.P. for Essex East and soon to be appointed secretary of state, leaves the impression that his meeting with Croll was accidental, but in fact, he sought Croll out to convey Mackenzie King's endorsement of Croll's candidacy in the forthcoming federal election. At the time, it appeared that Tim Buck, leader of the Communist party of Canada, was going to run in Toronto's Spadina riding. David Croll was judged the only Liberal who could beat him.

Political developments in Canada would mean the almost immediate end of Croll's career as a soldier. When the election was called for 11 June 1945, he made his way to Canada and did not look back. He resigned from the army as a confirmed lieutenant colonel effective 30 July 1945, a few months less than six years after first enlisting as a private.

There wasn't much room for sentimental farewells in the army, but Croll did get a pleasant note from Maj. Gen. A. E. Walford, the adjutant general, on 31 July 1945, part of which read:

> I am sending you this personal note to express the sincere appreciation of the Minister and of the Army Council for very useful services which you have performed in the interests of the Canadian Army on Active Service in this war.

> On behalf of the Army, I express deep appreciation, sincere thanks and every good wish for health and success.

Perhaps this was merely a form letter, but it would be nice to think that it was not.

SEVEN

The Honourable Gadfly
for Spadina

CROLL WAS SERVING WITH THE BRITISH LIBERATION
Army as a staff officer 1, civil affairs, in northwestern Europe
late in 1944 when he was formally asked by the local Liberal
association in Toronto's Spadina riding to be a candidate in
the forthcoming election. Since the Nineteenth Parliament
had been elected in 1940, it was evident that the five-year
limit would soon expire, but dissolution did not occur until 16
April 1945. Arthur Roebuck, who had become the federal
member of the House of Commons for Toronto's Trinity riding in the election of 26 May 1940, was instrumental in securing the nomination for Croll. Roebuck, who had been
named to the Senate two days after dissolution, had taken
over the management of the Liberal campaign in Ontario for
the 1945 campaign at Mackenzie King's request.

On 28 January 1945, Croll stated that he was prepared to
be a candidate, although he would not abandon his military
duties until the war in Europe was over. He then began to
fight his way through the jungle of red tape in the Canadian
Army for the authorization of political leave. Part of the military procedure involved the insertion of a declaration of
Croll's intent in the *Canada Gazette*. A formal notice was also
published in the *Toronto Daily Star* by Arthur Roebuck and

Sam Factor on 8 February. The upshot was that Croll was granted political leave from 15 May to 13 June and flew back to Canada to begin his campaign.

From a personal point of view, he did not want to leave Windsor, but the avenues of political advancement there were blocked off and Spadina offered a new challenge. In a number of ways, Spadina was a microcosm of urban industrial Canada, not unlike Windsor-Walkerville. The needle trades dominated the economic life of this district. Kensington Market added colour. The southern part of the riding was working class; the north end, mainly a high-rent area. Outside the industrialized section, there were white-collar workers, businessmen and a multitude of small retail stores. The workers were predominantly Jews but included an amalgam of Italians, Ukrainians, Poles, Slovaks and others. There were about 115,000 people in Spadina in the late 1940s, many of them politically active and radical in outlook.

Both Sam Factor, who had represented Spadina federally since 1930 but was now a county court judge, and Roebuck were of great help to Croll in building up his organization. So much so that Croll's campaign was short and relatively easy, lasting less than a month. It later amused him to claim that all he had to do was put on his uniform and walk through the streets meeting the people. In fact, a great many people contributed to his success. A delegation of Italians from Windsor even travelled to Toronto to help. Croll was also fortunate in being able to win the support of talented people like Sam Shapiro, the Yiddish actor and intellectual, who was to work long and faithfully as an organizer for Croll in all his campaigns. The result on 11 June was:

David A. Croll (L)	17,976
George Hees (PC)	10,846
Sam Carr (LPP)[1]	10,050
Mrs. Kay Morris (CCF)	2,769

Tim Buck, the head of the Communists in Canada, perhaps because of Croll's candidacy in Spadina, had switched to Toronto's Trinity riding, leaving the redoubtable Sam Carr to run in his place. They both lost. An editorial in the *Globe and Mail* rejoiced:

In Spadina the Communist candidate was the party's chief or-ganizer for Canada, Mr. Sam Carr. He, too, ran third, with Major George Hees, the Progressive Conservative, a young and enterprising wounded veteran, making a hard, clean run for second place against the winner, Lt. Col. David Croll.

Col. Croll, who joined the army on the outbreak of the war, as a private, while he was a Liberal member of the Ontario legislature and Mayor of Windsor made a first-class run. This new member from Toronto did not get his commission until he was overseas. From private to lieutenant-colonel and elec-tion to the House of Commons has been the Croll career dur-ing the war. He is an able experienced parliamentarian, and should be a first-rate member.

It was gratifying that a member of Canada's Army and a mem-ber of Canada's air force [w/c Lawrence Skey, a Conserva-tive] should be the ones to defeat the Communists.[2]

Within a few months of the election, Croll came as close as he was ever to come to securing a cabinet appointment. To-wards the end of August, Prime Minister King was considering the restructuring of his cabinet and sought the advice of Ian Mackenzie, M.P. for Vancouver Centre and minister of veter-ans affairs. On 23 August, King recorded part of his discussion in his diary:

He [Mackenzie] said he would need some help in administer-ing the Department. He had spoken of possible [David] Croll as an Assistant Minister. I told him our thoughts were running on the same lines. I really felt it would be best for him to stay in the Department, to complete the work as he has said, but instead of Croll, I would suggest Bridges, making him a Minister without Portfolio and making him Parliamentary Assistant as well. Mackenzie said this was perfectly satisfactory to him.[3]

For some reason King changed his mind, and on 29 August 1945, H. F. G. Bridges, the newly elected M.P. for the New Brunswick riding of York-Sunbury, was appointed minister of fisheries. Bridges had been Croll's second-in-command as a civil affairs officer in Europe, and by coincidence they had been discharged from the army on the same day. Unfortunately, Bridges' political career was cut short by his death on 10 August 1947.

There were occasions, and this change of heart was one of them, when Croll was disappointed and displeased with Mackenzie King, but despite this, he retained a deep admiration for the old Liberal leader. Croll did not understand King very well and was never close to him, but he looked up to King as the Liberal philosopher par excellence who had sponsored reforms throughout his career.

If Croll felt any bitterness towards King, it was soon forgotten. On the fifth anniversary of King's death, on 22 July 1955, there was a wreath-laying ceremony at Mount Pleasant cemetery in Toronto. Two of the main participants were Croll and Senator A. L. Woodrow. On this occasion Croll is reported to have said:

This pilgrimage will become an annual event for those who believe in the Liberal tradition and wish to keep green the memory of that great Canadian who gave Liberalism inspiration and substance.

He was also quoted as declaring with equal optimism that with the passing of the years, the full stature of King's greatness had become even more clearly defined and that time had added lustre to his memory.[4]

At the outset of the 1945 election campaign, Croll established a residence in Spadina (in a somewhat seedy hotel), but this was a cosmetic, not a legal, requirement. He actually lived in one of the grander hotels downtown while he tried to find suitable accommodation for his family. Despite the critical postwar housing shortage, he found a spacious apartment a little north of the riding boundary and was able to move his wife and daughters from Windsor. Throughout his tenure as M.P. for Spadina, he maintained a constituency office, which was open one week day and on Saturdays so that people with problems could reach him. He had to pay for this out of his own pocket. It would be many years before such facilities were to be supported by public funds.

He also undertook to re-establish a law practice. Being a member of Parliament was not very lucrative (four thousand dollars for each session of more than sixty-five days), and he had just spent six lean years in the army. Also, because of the vagaries of political life, he needed a refuge if the voters at some point decided to reject him. In 1947, he joined a former crown attorney, Norman Borins, who had graduated from Osgoode Hall in 1930, to form Croll and Borins. The firm was later expanded by the addition of another partner, J. Richard Shiff. Shiff later became chairman of Bramalea Limited, the real estate developer.

The first postwar Parliament met on 6 September 1945, and Croll's maiden speech in the House of Commons was on a motion by Angus MacInnis, the CCF member for Vancouver East, that the Old Age Pensions Act should be amended by lowering the pensionable age to sixty years, by increasing the amount of the pension to permit pensioners to live in health and self-respect and by eliminating the means test. Croll supported MacInnis's proposals with ardour:

A more prominent place must be given to Old Age Pensions because it is becoming an acute problem. There are a great number of objections to the Old Age Pensions Act now on the statute books. The first one is the means test. Because it is unparliamentary I cannot say what I think about that test. . . . People who look on that [Old Age Pensions] as charity are mistaken. People who look on it as a burden are mistaken. It is a long overdue dividend to the pioneers and builders of this country.[5]

Croll went on to stress the related need for health insurance and unemployment insurance. He emphasized that it was essential to look at social services from a broad point of view, a theme he was to pursue for many years.

Judging by the official indexes that purported to measure the cost of living, the Canadian government had very successfully controlled wartime prices for consumer goods. The postwar relaxation of controls, however, combined with the explosive growth of consumer demand, inevitably led to a worrisome increase in prices. There was a public outcry, along with some sharp criticism of the government in the House of Commons, particularly by the CCF. The government's response was to propose the establishment of a Special Committee to Inquire into Price Increases and Matters Pertaining Thereto early in February 1948.[6] Croll was not satisfied with this response. His constituency contained a high proportion of low-income families who were especially unhappy about rising food prices. Croll complained in the House of Commons:

Large-scale hardship has returned to my constituency, and the standard of living is declining. Insecurity and fear of the future constitute again a dominant factor in my constituency, and many of my constituents walk in the shadow of economic uncertainty, and are living from week to week. The main reason for this has been the violent rise in the prices of essential goods.[7]

On 14 January 1948, Croll had made a speech to the Trades and Labour Congress in Toronto in which he suggested, among other things, a complete, open and thorough investigation of the current high prices.[8] There was a lot of talk about price gouging, and it was clear from Croll's comments that he wanted it exposed in all its infamy. The government's proposal to appoint a special committee to inquire into price increases did nothing to pacify him. "I have groped for an answer and I know of no other answer in this emergency of trying to hold the line than to restore necessary controls on essential goods."[9] He then went on to argue for a reduction in the federal sales tax and for the reimposition of the wartime excess profits tax. Croll's aggressive attitude encouraged *Saturday Night* to burst into poetry:

SHORT DISCIPLINARY POEM

Mister Croll
Wants price control
Mister King
Wants no such thing[10]

After a lengthy debate, the government's motion to appoint an investigative committee was adopted, but Croll was notably absent from its roster. He had broken ranks on this issue, and this did not commend him to his political masters.

Croll had encountered the devastating effects of illness on the unemployed and poor, both when he was mayor of Windsor and when he was responsible for public welfare in Ontario in the mid-1930s. The Liberal platform of 1919 had called for some kind of sickness insurance, and interest in the subject was widespread, particularly as a result of experiments in the western provinces after 1935 with various kinds of government-sponsored schemes covering hospital and other medical costs. In addition, various private agencies were involved in prepaid health care. Although participation of the federal government was handicapped by constitutional obstacles, some progress was made with the introduction of the national health program in 1948, which provided substantial grants to the provinces to bolster their health care systems. Health insurance was a popular topic in the House of Commons after the war, and members such as Croll and Stanley Knowles kept needling the government to press on.

In December 1952, Croll presented a long and detailed plea for action. One of his arguments was that health insurance plans characteristically encouraged the expansion of hospitals and other medical facilities. He pointed to the rapid increase in medical personnel in Britain since the introduction of comprehensive health care in 1948. Some of the Canadian statistics quoted by Croll were disturbing. Despite Canada's high standard of living, the infant mortality rate was only the twelfth lowest in the world. Armed forces medical examinations showed that more than 50 per cent of prospective recruits were unfit for service, and Croll concluded that the proportion of the total population suffering from health problems was probably even higher. Croll's proposal was forthright:

> In common with many others in this country I believe our answer is to be found in some plan of national health insurance underwritten by the dominion and administered by the provinces for the benefit of all Canadians.[11]

Another of Croll's constant themes was old age pensions. As already mentioned, he was sharply critical of the continued application of the means test.[12] In order to appreciate his attitude, it may be useful to review the main aspects of old-age pensions in Canada up to the time Croll became a member of the federal Parliament. The original federal legislation passed in 1927 provided for pensions of $20 a month to those seventy and over, subject to certain residence requirements, provided their maximum outside income did not exceed $125 a year. Initially the cost was shared equally with the provinces, which in turn passed on a share to the municipalities, but in later amendments to the legislation during the Bennett regime, the federal share was increased to 75 per cent. In 1943, action was taken under the War Measures Act to raise the pension to $25 a month. In 1947, the government proposed to raise the pension by another $5 a month and to increase the amount permitted under the means test to $50 a month, including the pension. Taking into account provincial supplements, an individual with no other income could get $600 a year. And shortly before the federal election of 1949, the amount of the pension was increased to $40 a month. By early 1950, however, criticism of the means test was so widespread that the government was forced to act. At the end of March, a special joint committee of the Senate and the House of Commons on Old Age Security, was set up at the instance of the minister of national health and welfare, Paul Martin. The co-chairmen were Jean Lesage and Senator J. H. King. [13] Among the members from the House of Commons were Croll, William Benidickson, Donald Fleming and Stanley Knowles. The committee held fifty-two sittings during its life of roughly four months.

Naturally, the means test was a source of discord, and Croll, Fleming and Knowles were designated a subcommittee to resolve this issue. Croll was keen to win over Knowles, the CCF member for Winnipeg North Centre, to the proposal that the government pay thirty dollars a month to those seventy and over, with no means test. The agreement of the CCF both in the committee and in the House of Commons was important to the government. After some hard bargaining, Knowles agreed to support a universal pension of forty dollars a month for those seventy and over and a pension subject to a means test for those between sixty-five and sixty-nine, with the provinces sharing the cost of this latter group. Fleming, a prominent Toronto Tory, dissented. Nevertheless, on 28 June 1950, the joint committee recommended the scheme agreed to by Croll and Knowles.[14] It proved necessary, however, to amend the British North America Act to allow the federal government to deal with old age pensions in the manner proposed, but the requisite changes were passed by the British Parliament on 31 May 1951, and the new rules governing pensions came into effect on 1 January 1952. Thus, Croll's bête noire, the means test, was eliminated for a major group of old age pensioners, and its abolition for everyone over sixty-five was not far off.

In the spring of 1953, Milton Gregg, the minister of labour, introduced the Fair Employment Practices Bill in the House of Commons. The aim of this bill was to prohibit discrimination in employment and membership in trade unions because of race, national origin, colour or religion. The application of the bill, of course, was limited to fields under federal jurisdiction. Gregg was generous in acknowledging Croll's support for this legislation:

> I think it is only fair to say that several members of the house have stressed the importance of the government taking some action in this field. I do feel that it would be wrong in introducing the bill if I did not acknowledge one voice from this side of the house that has been forceful, consistent and eloquent in its demands for action against discrimination for many more years than I have been a member of the house. I refer of course to the voice of the hon. member for Spadina

(Mr. Croll). I wish to express to him my warmest thanks for all he has done in the past to help prepare the ground to make possible the introduction of this bill at this time. I am sure there are many Canadians outside the house who would want me to make this public expression of gratitude to the hon. member for Spadina on their behalf.[15]

Croll acknowledged Gregg's kind comments and observed:

Intolerance and discrimination are the two sides of the coin of infamy which has been current for too long. It is the duty of all of us, nations no less than individuals, to wipe out this base currency which is a constant threat to our freedom.[16]

Croll prodded the government consistently on a range of mainly social issues, pressing as hard as he could for reform. Some of the political commentators of the day thought he might have hurt his standing in the party. George Bain observed in 1955 in his "Ottawa Letter" in the *Globe and Mail*:

In the years that he was in the Commons Mr. Croll consistently was in the van of the party in advocating the introduction of social legislation. There is a sizeable body of opinion within the Government that the ordinary MP's highest duty is to conform gracefully, and Mr. Croll's proddings were not unanimously well received.[17]

Conversely, the government regularly called on Croll to help out with some difficult issue as a negotiator, a committee member or committee chairman. His political agility and skill were invaluable assets to the government, even though his goading may have ruffled some feathers. For example, following the outbreak of the Korean War, when the St. Laurent government found itself under relentless attack in the House of Commons for the alleged mismanagement of the disposal and procurement of army materiel, a special committee of the House of Commons on defence expenditures was struck on 13 November 1951 with Croll as its chairman. His job was to defuse the issue and get the extravagant charges of Opposition leader George Drew and other Progressive Conservative M.P.'s off the front pages. The committee gathered evidence on the procurement of many items, such as teapots, socks, neckties and battle dress. Excesses were exposed, such as an order for 63,000 long-handled serving forks, and corrective measures initiated. Most often, however, the amounts of public money involved were trivial. Under Croll's skillful chairmanship, everyone had his day in court and the committee was able to produce a report that had a soothing effect.

Then, on 12 October 1951, an anonymous letter to the RCMP alleged certain irregularities in transactions between personnel of the Army Works Service detachment in Camp Petawawa and a company dealing in scrap metal in Brockville. A joint investigation by the RCMP and the Provost Corps exposed a conspiracy among several members of the engineer's detachment to defraud the army through the improper disposal of scrap. Both criminal and civil charges were laid against a number of soldiers, civilians and companies. A good part of the materiel that had been illegally disposed of was recovered, and the estimated loss after recoveries amounted to roughly $35,000.[18]

The situation uncovered at Camp Petawawa was indicative of an administrative breakdown, although it was noted later that the emergency arising out of Canada's participation in the Korean War had strained army control and accounting procedures. The minister of national defence, Brooke Claxton, announced in the House of Commons in April 1952 that he had invited George S. Currie, a partner in the firm of McDonald, Currie and Company, chartered accountants, of

Montreal to investigate the activities of the Army Works Service, including security and accounting practices, at Camp Petawawa and elsewhere.[19] During the preliminary investigations of the Army Provost Corps, some time had been spent checking out the allegation that horses had been hired by army personnel and put on the payroll under the names of fictitious labourers. Despite the fact that this proved untrue, the Currie report repeated the charge. The whole notion was a source of great merriment to the press and the Opposition politicians, but the humorous aspects of horses on the payroll escaped the government. The prime minister gave a solemn assurance that, "There were no false names on the payroll and no horses on the payroll."[20] But the truth didn't seem to matter; the very phrase "horses on the payroll" was enough for the Opposition. St. Laurent undertook to divert them in mid-January 1953 by appointing a new select committee, again under the chairmanship of David Croll. The question was whether he could repeat his earlier success.

At the first open meeting of the committee on 29 January 1953, Brig. W. J. Lawson, Judge Advocate General of the Department of National Defence, gave the committee a detailed account of the events at Camp Petawawa and the punishments that had been handed out by the civilian and military authorities. Lawson denied the entertaining invention about horse on the payroll. He was followed by Currie, who dealt in great detail with his findings and recommendations.[21] Before long the committee was completely absorbed in technical details concerning such things as cost overruns at various military sites across Canada, and the Currie Report began to fade into the background in precisely the way that Croll and his Liberal colleagues on the committee intended.

In its report, the committee dealt gently with such sins as its findings had exposed. Horses on the payroll were not among them:

The great majority of the accounting irregularities listed were found to be the result of failure to comply with the proper accounting and administrative procedures in strict accordance with the various regulations and instructions. These omissions had largely resulted from the urgency of Defence requirements following the outbreak of hostilities in Korea, the vastly increased volume of work due to Canadian commitments to NATO and the United Nations and the difficulty of securing adequate and well-trained staff. To some extent the importance of accomplishing the work had been placed ahead of the desirability of reaching administrative perfection.[22]

Croll had again disarmed the government's critics, assuring the House of Commons that whereas things were not totally satisfactory in the Army Works Service, perfection is not of this world.

There were some protests, however, about Croll's conduct of the inquiry. George Hees, Conservative M.P. for Toronto's Broadview riding, told the *Globe and Mail*:

The defence expenditure committee has been a deliberate farce from start to finish. It has not been permitted to examine the vast majority of defence items, and has spent its time on minor matters of little importance.[23]

He also claimed, with some truth, that Croll proceeded to write his own report without consulting any of the other committee members.

Perhaps in recognition of these successes, early in 1954 Croll was designated chairman of the very important House of Commons Standing Committee on Banking and Commerce. Three bills had been referred to the committee for study. The first of these concerned somewhat technical but vital aspects of Canada's housing legislation dealing with insured mortgage loans and limited-dividend housing.[24] The next bill involved some amendments to the Bank of Canada Act. The final piece of legislation dealt with the decennial revision of the Bank Act. The changes proposed in the Bank Act were minor except for removing the prohibition against loans on residential real estate. Croll's committee held twenty-nine sessions, plus three supplementary sessions, related to the Public Service Superannuation Act. All told, there were about a thousand pages of recorded evidence. On 1 June 1954, the *Toronto Daily Star* reported:

> At a recent Liberal caucus, Mr. St. Laurent took the unusual step of congratulating him [Croll] for his work as chairman of the important banking and commerce committee, which this session handled the amendments to the Bank Act and the National Housing Act.

The introduction of legislation in 1946 to recognize the existence of Canadian citizens was overdue. For many years, nonaliens in Canada were either British subjects or Canadian nationals, but the legal concept of Canadian citizenship was not recognized. The bill provided a complex set of legal rules defining Canadian citizens and describing the naturalization process. For some, such as Croll, the citizenship bill stirred deep emotions. He said in the House of Commons:

> For forty-one years of my forty-six I have lived in this country, have enjoyed liberties and opportunities it has given me. I have gladly allowed myself to be assimilated into its community. What little service it has allowed me to give, I have proudly given. Yet I remain a new Canadian. I am not a native-born; I am a naturalized citizen. Behind me remains, and occasionally I hear, the reminder of those cold years when, from the wrong side of the tracks, this new Canadian

could only look across enviously at the warmly-lighted windows of those who enjoyed Canadian birthright and who so casually accepted the high privileges which were theirs from the cradle on.[25]

Croll emphasized that he had no patience with hyphenated Canadianism:

I suggest also that we call our people Canadians and forget that destructive hyphen we are so wont to use. Surely after all these years we are no longer English or Irish or French or German or Hebrew or Ukrainian Canadians? Surely the people of these national backgrounds need no longer huddle protectively among others of the same descent, keeping alive their immigrant ways and customs only because they have not yet been accepted into the larger community which apparently is not yet ready to avow its Canadianism.[26]

Croll has never displayed any enthusiasm for multiculturalism, despite its vogue in recent years. He would rather dwell on the privileges of Canadian citizenship and the goal of Canadian unity. In any case, it was a happy day for Croll when the new Canadian Citizenship Act came into force on 1 January 1947.

In the spring of 1946, when the House of Commons was considering the citizenship bill, John Diefenbaker, then Conservative M.P. for Lake Centre, Saskatchewan, proposed an amendment that would require every certificate of citizenship to include a bill of rights. Croll joined in the debate and called on the government for positive steps:

I feel that a clear and concise statement on the matter of citizenship rights is long overdue, and I think it is a good time for us to consider a bill of rights which will act as a bulwark for the cause of free men.[27]

He noted that Canada's record had been stained, specifically mentioning the Duplessis padlock law in Quebec and the defunct Section 98 of the Criminal Code, which had allowed the indiscriminate deportation of radicals or suspected radicals during the anticommunist hysteria following World War I. He was highly critical of the forced relocation of the Japanese from British Columbia in 1942 and pointed to the arbitrary use of government power in the espionage investigations following the defection of the Soviet cypher clerk Igor Gouzenko. Although he did not believe the Diefenbaker proposal was adequate, he warned that the issue would not die: "The government is notified that we intend that it shall in due time produce a bill of rights which will be acceptable not only to members of the house but also to the country at large."[28] This intervention by Croll marked the beginning of his long friendship with John Diefenbaker. Apart from this, there was a special link between Croll and the future Conservative prime minister. A relative of Diefenbaker's first wife, Edna, who had served with Croll in the army, had been killed in action. The two men often talked and exchanged confidences. It was Croll's assessment, however, that while Diefenbaker's populism might one day gain him the prime minister's office, it would not keep him there.

On 24 March 1952, Diefenbaker suggested that consideration be given to introducing a bill or declaration of rights primarily to guarantee the rights of individuals or minorities. He opened by acknowledging that Croll had deferred to him:

May I at the outset acknowledge the courtesy of the hon. member for Spadina (Mr. Croll) who was considerate enough to allow my motion to be on the order paper ahead of his, and who declined to proceed the other day with his own motion. That is something I sincerely appreciate.[29]

Diefenbaker noted that the first time he had brought the need for a bill of rights to the attention of the House, his proposal was too narrow. On this occasion, he was seeking to provide for a bill of rights that would apply to all Canadians. Croll spoke in support of Diefenbaker's motion and expressed agreement with his eloquent exposition. Croll noted that if Canada's support of the United Nations Declaration of Human Rights in 1948 meant anything, then the government should do something about it. There was, he claimed, a crying need to restate formally the principles of individual freedom: "It is beyond question that one of the fundamental freedoms in any bill of rights is the freedom from discrimination on grounds of race, colour or creed."[30] He summarized his position by saying:

> What I want in a bill of rights is freedom within the law depending on two basic principles. First, that the individual may do and say what he believes, so long as he does not transgress the substantive law of the land. Second, the public authorities may only do those things which are authorized by common law or statute. It is within this framework that our Canadian bill of rights can be constructed.[31]

Diefenbaker's proposal was shelved on the motion of the minister of citizenship and immigration, Walter Harris, on 24 March 1952.[32]

Diefenbaker pursued the issue again in February 1955. Related motions by Croll and the CCF's national leader, M. J. Coldwell, were again withdrawn to give Diefenbaker a clear path. However, the government did not look upon this question with favour, apparently believing that the adoption of such a declaration would indicate a lack of faith in Parliament. Or at least that was the view John Diefenbaker attributed to Stuart Garson, the minister of justice.[33] Diefenbaker finally had his triumph in 1960, when the Bill of Rights he and Croll and Coldwell had sponsored for so many years came into force with much fanfare.

Not unrelated to the question of a Canadian bill of rights was the forced evacuation of Japanese Canadians from the coastal areas of British Columbia following Pearl Harbor. Then, in August 1944, Mackenzie King announced the policy of relocating the evacuees across Canada. In addition to the original evacuation order, another passed in 1943 prohibited Japanese from entering British Columbia without an RCMP permit.[34]

Not until the spring of 1948 did the government introduce legislation to revoke the 1943 Order in Council, which was to take effect on 1 April 1949. The perpetuation of discrimination against the Japanese for four years after the end of hostilities was a sad commentary on attitudes towards civil liberties at that time and contrasted sharply with the situation in the United States, where restrictions on the Japanese had been lifted eight months before VJ Day. To Croll, the whole business was lamentable. He vehemently attacked government policy in the House of Commons, which doubtless did little to endear him to the prime minister or the other ministers directly involved in the government's decision:

> Mr. Chairman, in speaking to this bill one can say for it that at long last the end of official discrimination against the Japanese in Canada is in sight. This bill, tardy and ungenerous though it is, at least draws the line of April 1, 1949, and no farther. I hope it marks the close of a chapter in Canadian history that we shall not be very proud to write in our school books.

I am not going to say very much today by way of valedictory. I spoke and used whatever influence I had against the government's action against Japanese of Canadian citizenship, but the government persisted in its view, although whatever justification there may have been for it came to an end at least two and a half years ago with the end of the war.

I can only say this. As one who was highly privileged to serve my country during the war I hang my head in shame before my comrades in arms of Japanese ancestry. As a member of this house I can neither forgive nor justify the wrong that has been done to a blameless people. As a firm believer in democracy I must say that I think we betrayed the fundamental principle of democracy which I consider to be equality. As a human being I say that we have committed an offence in passing judgement on our fellow men solely on the basis of blood and race. As a member of a minority race I say to the minority people, be ever on your guard.

In Canada there is no room for the doctrine of racial supremacy, nor is there any room for second-class citizenship. I only hope that my country will never again put me in the position where I have to stammer forth some sort of explanation or apology for the action which the government has taken. Our treatment of Canadians of Japanese ancestry was in my opinion wrong in principle and demeaning in its application both to the Japanese and to ourselves.

It is my sincere hope that Canada will never again be guilty of official discrimination against any race or creed. Liberty is indivisible. It seems to me that if the humblest citizen of Canada is not free there is no freedom in this country for any of us.

> I said that I was not going to say much about the bill. To all
> that is contained in this bill I say good-bye and good riddance.
> I hope we shall never see the like of it again.[35]

If Croll's attack had no effect on the government's thinking, what more could he do? Much, as it turned out. He issued
a public invitation to displaced Japanese to move to Spadina
and convened a meeting of the various ethnic groups in his
constituency to ask them to welcome the Japanese as new
neighbours. This they gladly did. Many years later, the Japanese in Toronto honoured Croll for his advocacy of their cause.
On 15 May 1977, the centennial celebration marking the arrival of the first Japanese in Canada, Croll was guest speaker
at a dinner for six hundred people at the Prince Hotel in Toronto, where in recognition of his efforts on behalf of the Japanese, he was presented with a painting by the Nisei artist
Kazuo Pamasaki.

Croll's record in looking after his Spadina constituents was
exemplary. Since he was the only Liberal member from Toronto elected in 1945, he was called on for help by troubled
people, especially by veterans and immigrants, all over the
city. There was so much work that he was assigned two extra
secretaries to handle his correspondence. In July 1947, the
Trinity Liberal Association named Croll the most outstanding
member of the House of Commons in the last session.[36] He was
also much in demand, as he had been from the early stages of
his political career, as a public speaker. And his success in political combat was so remarkable that many Liberal candidates
wanted the benefit of his coattails.

One contest that commanded considerable public attention
was the by-election in Montreal's Cartier riding in 1947,
which was called after the sitting member, Fred Rose, had
been sentenced to prison for espionage activities on behalf of
the Soviet Union. It was important for the Liberals to break

Senator Croll: "We've opened doors that never again will be closed."

Minka Croll with three sons in uniform during World War II. *Left to right:* Maurice, David and Leo.

Hillel and Minka Croll in middle age.

Croll as a neophyte lawyer in Windsor, c. 1925.

Horseplay with Jack Dempsey, 1934.

Constance Croll presenting a bouquet to Queen Elizabeth, 6 June 1939. King George VI and Mackenzie King are in the background; Sarah Croll is in the foreground.

Lieutenant Croll to his daughters from somewhere in England, June 1941.

Croll (*second from left, second row*) with his classmates at the Royal Military College (Sandhurst), October 1940.

Croll eyeing George Currie, House of Commons Defence Expenditure Committee, 1954.

Louis St. Laurent greeting Sarah Croll, c. mid-1950s.

Croll receiving an award from the governor general, Vincent Massey, late 1950s.

Croll with his mother and wife at his installation in the Senate, 1955.

The children of Hillel and Minka Croll. *Left to right:* Samuel, Evelyn, Maurice, Leo, David and Cecil.

Sarah Croll, 1961.

Croll with his bosom friend, Senator Arthur Roebuck, c. 1962.

Croll on the main road of his birthplace, Teterina, U.S.S.R., 1965.

Croll in the foreground at the Liberal nominating convention, 1968. Pierre Trudeau is standing on his right.

Croll with Menachem Begin, 1978.

Memorial parade, September 1982.

David Arnold Croll, May 1982. *Photograph by Michael Bedford.*

the hold of the Labour Progressive (Communist) party in this riding. Croll was called in to help. Maurice Hartt, the Liberal candidate, won with a majority of 2,720. Croll's efforts on his behalf were warmly commended by Mackenzie King:

> In a letter just received from Mr. Bertrand [postmaster general and member for Montreal's Laurier riding], Mr. Bertrand speaks of the splendid services which you rendered the Party in the recent by-election in Cartier.

> This line is just to add my thanks to those of other of the Ministers and our friends generally for your contribution to the success of the campaign. I cannot think of any recent by-election more significant or one the result of which has put more heart into our men.

> I shall hope to renew this word of thanks on my return to Ottawa. Meanwhile, my kindest remembrances and all good wishes to you.[37]

Croll and the Liberal party were riding high as the 1949 election approached. It was the best of times. Louis St. Laurent, at age sixty-seven, had succeeded Mackenzie King as prime minister on 15 November 1948. He had been a Liberal cabinet minister since early in December 1941, but most of his adult life had been devoted to the law. Although there was some muttering that he lacked experience in partisan politics, he was regarded with affection and trust by a great many Canadians in every region. There was a spirit of optimism in the country that reinforced the satisfaction of the people with the prime minister and his party.

When the date was finally set for 27 June, the prospect did not alarm Croll. He had built an impressive record in Parliament. One of his election brochures, entitled "Dave Croll said these things in Parliament," quoted him as follows:

"I cannot picture this country without a strong and responsible trade union movement. . . they are the very core of democracy and we must preserve them."

9th October, 1945.

"In this country the seniority of the worker has become a property right in his job."

15th December, 1945.

"If in this House we can formulate a sane yet generous immigration policy we shall be giving the most direct assistance to the victims of this war. . . . Humanity calls upon us to share our good fortune with those people who are not ungrateful, who are not unappreciative."

3rd April, 1946.

"I entertain no belief that loyalty can be divided—so much to the state and so much to another organism."

9th April, 1946.

"From the date the Citizenship Act is proclaimed there should be no longer new Canadians or old Canadians—we all belong."

9th April, 1946.

"The present unemployment insurance benefits are inadequate. . . . An increase of 50% is warranted."

4th July, 1946.

"I am whole-heartedly and everlastingly opposed to discrimination on the basis of race or creed, or to any other discrimination."

24th April, 1947.

"We are now living in an age that calls for a new social deal."
18th June, 1947.

"I have always been opposed to the means test. It is archaic
and ungenerous."

18th June, 1947.

"Until we are prepared to guarantee the freedom of the individual in a broadly conceived bill of rights. . . . We shall go ill-
armed into the great ideological conflict."

12th April, 1948.

"I dislike and distrust communism because it is dictorial [*sic*],
because it is tyrannical and because it is totalitarian."

25th May, 1948.

"Health Insurance in this country is not extravagant nor is it
back-door Socialism, but if it is either it is still necessary."

3rd February, 1949.

Croll also found that some of the bread he had cast upon the
waters was coming back sandwiches. A small delegation of the
Japanese community in Spadina came to see him to tell him
that it was not necessary to canvass among them, that their
support was wholehearted.

One of the big efforts of the Liberals to enlighten Tory Toronto was a giant rally in Maple Leaf Gardens on 21 July. The
principal speaker was St. Laurent, but the stage was crowded

with the luminaries of the Liberal party—even Mackenzie King emerged from retirement for the occasion. St. Laurent made a dramatic pitch to the multitude and in his speech spoke warmly of Croll: "I first appeal to the electors of Spadina to insure the re-election of our good friend David Croll, who has been so tireless in advancing their interests and will continue to do so."[38]

The outcome in Spadina cannot have been in much doubt, because Croll romped home. The results were:

David A. Croll (L)	23,652
Dr. Willard Box (PC)	9,407
William White (CCF)	5,969

Croll's majority was the fourth largest in Canada. Outside of Spadina, the Liberals swept the country. The final tally was:

Liberal	190
Progressive Conservative	41
CCF	13
Social Credit	10
Other	8
Total	262

Croll received enthusiastic good wishes from Mackenzie King, who wrote, "I was delighted at your return to the House of Commons at yesterday's election. This is just a line to extend to you my heartiest congratulations. What a magnificent victory!"[39] Croll's acknowledgement was also generous:

I was delighted to hear from you and to have your good wishes, which I prize very highly. I know who was the builder of the present victory, and the public does also. I hope you are long spared in good health and happiness.[40]

Croll was the spearhead of a campaign that won seven seats for the Liberals in Toronto and the Yorks out of a total of fifteen. The blitz led by St. Laurent was doubtless influential, but Croll's organizational and political skills were major factors in the success of the Liberal contingent.

St. Laurent had been fortunate in taking over the stewardship of a healthy economy. The worrisome price increases that followed the lifting of wartime price controls had subsided, and consumer prices were increasing at what seem in retrospect a moderate pace. Some economists were concerned about a possible recession, but the outbreak of hostilities in Korea in 1950 banished these fears. Immigration reached unprecedented levels. Unemployment was low. Between 1949 and 1955, the gross national product nearly doubled.

The result was that the St. Laurent government was able to enter a period of extraordinary legislative achievement. Because the country was prosperous, it was practical to make significant progress in such areas as old age security, unemployment insurance and health grants. And in the 1952 budget, it proved possible to cut the level of income taxes appreciably.

When Parliament was dissolved on 12 June 1953, the outlook for the Liberals was again rosy. Because Croll's seat in Spadina was under lock and key, he was called on to help out in seventeen other constituencies during the campaign. It was a tribute to his standing in the party and a recognition of his political prowess, but the extra effort drained him both physically and mentally.

St. Laurent's appeal to the electors was quiet and dignified. His campaign started in Windsor on 22 June and climaxed with another giant rally in Maple Leaf Gardens on 7 August. In an obviously partisan news story, the *Toronto Daily Star* summarized the prime minister's message:

He was telling them earnestly and in quiet language without the least attempt to dramatize himself or dazzle the voters, that

he and his colleagues had done their best, that they appreciated the trust and that they were prepared to carry on to the
limit of their ability. He was telling them by his manner that
there are issues which one must approach with humility, and
that even as he reached the climax of a stirring campaign—for
that it had been—he would not attempt to belittle those issues
by boasts or levity or toy with them by extravagant promises.[41]

Among the other speakers were trade and commerce minister
C. D. Howe, external affairs minister L. B. Pearson and
Croll. Croll can still recall the nervous strain of facing an audience of ten thousand. He was accustomed to political
speeches, but this was a new experience. He had had time for
only a sandwich before the rally, and it now rolled around like
a small cannonball in his stomach. Once he hit his stride,
however, he established a good rapport with the crowd, and
they laughed and cheered at his quips. He spoke glowingly of
St. Laurent, likening him to King and Laurier, and claimed
that Toronto was being transformed from a Tory stronghold to
a Liberal fortress.

In fact, Liberal fortunes in Toronto were improving greatly.
Three new ridings had been added since 1949, and when the
1953 results were known, out of a total of eighteen, the Liberals took ten; the Progressive Conservatives, seven; and the
CCF, one. When the new Parliament met on 12 November
1953, Croll's influence within the Liberal party had never
been stronger. Little did he suspect that he had run in his last
campaign, especially given the results in Spadina:

David A. Croll (L)	15,946
Averell Robinson (PC)	6,554
Elgin Blair (CCF)	3,270
Joshua Gershman (LPP)	1,938

The election was a fifth successive triumph for the Liberals:

Liberal	170
Progressive Conservative	51
CCF	23
Social Credit	15
Other	6
Total	265

In the summer of 1953, the *Toronto Daily Star* carried a story with the heading "Roebuck foresees Croll getting post in Cabinet."[42] Croll was a logical candidate—his credentials and political experience were excellent—but the summons did not come. There was a lot of speculation about the reasons. George Bain wrote that "a favourite guessing game in Ottawa concerns the reason for Croll's persistent failure to break away from the back benches."[43] The appointment of J. W. Pickersgill, previously a public servant, to a cabinet post in 1953, was seen by some as an affront to Toronto. Bain, a careful and well-informed observer, collected a variety of views on the reasons for Croll's treatment. He quoted George Hees, Croll's one-time adversary in Spadina:

> Comparing Dave Croll to the present members of the Cabinet, I think it would be the generally held opinion of all members of the House that he has more ability than two thirds of the Ministers. He is infinitely more capable than some. . . . [44]

The *Globe and Mail* raised the question of anti-Semitism in an editorial on 15 June 1953:

> In the last Federal election campaign Mr. St. Laurent gave what amounted to a promise that, if he were returned to

power, a Toronto member would be given ministerial rank. All who heard him assumed he had Mr. David Croll in mind. Mr. Croll is distinctly superior to Mr. Pickersgill in ability and experience; but he apparently has a racial stigma that disqualifies him in Mr. St. Laurent's eyes.

Bain conducted a miniature public opinion survey among some of his colleagues in the press gallery. This is what he found:

Among a representative group of parliamentary correspondents questioned recently, only one thought that Croll's being Jewish was no factor in his having remained a backbencher; some thought it was the dominant factor; most believed it was part of the reason. Others believe that Croll has been the victim of what might be called discrimination by procrastination: that he has been the subject of no decision rather than of an adverse decision. The theory follows these lines: no Jew has ever been a member of the federal cabinet; there remains here and there, notably in rural Quebec, considerable anti-Semitism which would, or could be, aroused at such an appointment; the necessity of making one is not pressing; hence it remains unmade.[45]

From 1945 to 1949, Croll, as the sole Liberal elected from Toronto, automatically exercised a veto over all federal patronage appointments in the area. Some people, forgetting his record as a minister in the Hepburn government, thought that he would use his influence to advance the interests of Jewish place seekers, but he continued scrupulously to avoid favouritism. This tactic not only made for good relations with his fellow Liberals, but also allowed him to open other, more important doors for Jews to serve on the high courts of Ontario and Quebec, where, through genuinely distinguished service, they in turn opened other doors.

EIGHT

A Friend in Need

Soon after he was elected to the House of Commons in 1945, Croll began a concerted attack on Canada's immigration policy. In December 1945, during the debate on the estimates of the Immigration Branch of the Department of Mines and Resources, he scolded the government and argued that Canada must open its heart and its doors to the thousands of orphans in Europe, whose immigration to Canada in time would pay great dividends. In the recent past, Canadian policy had been designed to exclude and restrict, but now the time had come to welcome new people:

> I cannot help saying to the minister that we have on our statute books at the present time a lot of racial nonsense. It is time to get it off the books. Racism is bad whether it comes from Canadians or Germans.[1]

While Croll did not refer explicitly to Canadian policy on Jewish immigration, there is no doubt he felt keenly about this issue, since the Canadian treatment of Jews seeking entry to Canada had been shameful. Prime Minister King had said that Canada would be willing to accept Jewish refugees, but the reality was that in most years between 1931 and 1945, the Jews admitted to Canada numbered only in the hundreds.[2]

In the spring of 1946, Croll again scorned the government's pallid excuses, which included the lack of ships and the need to conclude an agreement among governments concerning refugees:

> For almost thirty years we have allowed surface reasons to remain in the path of our own interests and in the interests of common humanity. The truth is that if we are looking for reasons for dodging the problem we can find them, but we must ask if they are fair to ourselves and fair to the rest of the world.[3]

He returned to the charge in August 1946, claiming that the government was merely nibbling at the problem of immigration and warning that Canada was seriously underpopulated. He said, "We have a country with unlimited resources and great potentialities, with an abundance of international good will, and yet for all purposes we are a land without people."[4]

In March 1947, Croll again complained about government inaction. He protested that "there has been a nation-wide demand from every walk of life for more people, yet the doors of this country have opened just a crack."[5] On the same occasion, he launched into an impassioned plea for the uprooted refugees in Europe:

> What is to be done with the tragic residue of men, women and children? Return to their homes is out of the question for a variety of reasons. In many instances their homes and possessions have been destroyed, through military operations. . . . Still others, notably Poles, Ukrainians and Baltic peoples who make up the majority of the displaced persons, cannot go back

because of the hostility of the governments which prevail in their homelands. . . .

The Jewish displaced persons, who number approximately fifteen per cent of the total, suffer most of these disabilities. They do not want to go back to the homelands, and they are not now wanted. Their homelessness poses an especially tragic problem because the war left [a] tragic residue of anti-Semitism in Europe.[6]

He continued:

Let us not dry up the wells of compassion. Every human instinct within us cries out for these people. Today the narrow gates of Canada are almost as hard to pass through as St. Peter's gates, and to the homeless of Europe they are the pearly gates on earth.[7]

Beginning in January 1947, there was a further slight loosening of the restrictions on refugees. An order in council admitted more relatives of Canadian residents, including widowed daughters and sisters with unmarried children under the age of eighteen. The age limit for orphans was raised from sixteen to eighteen, and experienced labourers in farming, mining and logging were considered admissible.[8] A further relaxation took place in May, when family units were admitted, excluding married children, as well as the betrothed of Canadian residents. On 1 May 1947, Prime Minister King explained his administration's new position:

The policy of the government is to foster the growth of the population of Canada by the encouragement of immigration. The government will seek by legislation, regulation and vigorous administration, to ensure the careful selection and permanent settlement of such numbers of immigrants as can be advantageously absorbed in our national economy.[9]

He stated that discriminatory provisions should be eliminated from the immigration laws, but not to the extent of permitting "large-scale immigration from the Orient," and acknowledged Canada's moral obligation to help meet the grievous problems of European refugees.

Early in June, provision was made for the admission of five thousand displaced persons.[10] Shortly thereafter this number was increased to ten thousand, and by October 1947, to twenty thousand. By April 1948, the quota had been raised to thirty thousand. This influx of immigrants was intended to alleviate domestic labour shortages, although a minority had relatives in Canada. Discrimination against Jews, however, persisted.

Croll's attacks on the government's immigration policies in the House of Commons and elsewhere led in a roundabout way to his first visit to the new state of Israel in the fall of 1948. Hundreds of letters had come to Croll complaining about anti-Semitic attitudes of Canadian officials dealing with displaced persons in the transit camps. J. A. Glen had replaced Thomas Crerar as the minister responsible and was receptive to Croll's complaints. A source in the Immigration Branch had been leaking documents to Croll, although he never did learn who his informant was. On the basis of this information, however, Croll was able to convince Glen that an investigation was warranted. Glen invited Croll to undertake an unpublicized tour of transit camps in Europe in the company of a departmental immigration inspector. Croll was to travel first to Israel so that the real purpose of the trip could be camouflaged, then fly to Frankfurt to meet his escort to begin their exploratory mission. Croll's investigation took him to

camps in Amberg, Linz and Bremen. He also visited Heidel-
berg and the Immigration Branch's administrative headquarters in Paris. The question was not so much whether there was
discrimination against Jewish refugees but whether these charges could be verified, and this often proved difficult, except in
Paris, where the evidence was clear. Part of the problem was
the difficulty of obtaining security clearances for the refugees.
Croll's understanding with Glen was that he would report to
him personally on his return and that there would be no written report. The abuses Croll outlined related to the discriminatory treatment not only of Jews but of Poles and Ukrainians
as well. Glen kept his part of the bargain by introducing the
charges necessary to eradicate improper practices.

By the end of 1949, Croll was paying compliments to the
cabinet for its more openhanded policy. In December, he
congratulated the government for its accomplishments since
the end of the war, claiming that Canada was the first overseas nation to establish a mass immigration program to help
the people in the European camps:

> We were the first from the new world to extend our hand to
> those unfortunates who were then rotting in the camps. . . .
> To date we have welcomed 90,000 immigrants to Canada,
> and the United States with her vast resources has only taken
> in 120,000. In the light of these figures I think we can be very
> proud, and we can give credit where credit is due.[11]

And so well did Glen's administrative reforms work that
Croll, during the 1949 federal election campaign, was able to
state that eleven thousand Jews had been admitted into Canada since the end of the war, more than to any other country
except Israel.[12] He was also able to describe Canada as one of
Israel's best friends.

Croll had absorbed Zionism through his pores. It was part of the credo of his parents, grandparents, uncles, aunts and cousins during his early years. No matter how geographically remote, many Jews in the Diaspora were spiritually close to the land of their ancestors. From early childhood, they had dinned into them the ancient Passover incantation "*Le shana haba be Yerushalayim*" (Next year in Jerusalem).

By 1945, Croll was the only Jew in the federal Parliament. Sam Factor had gone to the bench, Sam Jacobs was dead and A. A. Heaps had been defeated in 1940. He thus assumed a great responsibility in attempting to influence the course of Canadian policy on the subject of the state of Israel. In the summer of 1946, Croll was able to convince the House of Commons Standing Committee on External Affairs that it ought to hear several prominent representatives of Canadian Jewry discuss the future of Palestine. These representatives included Samuel J. Zacks and M. C. Garber, president and vice-president, respectively, of the United Zionist Council of Canada, and Herbert Mowat, executive director of the Canadian Palestine Committee. In introducing the witnesses, Croll explained:

> In the past ten years the Jews of Europe have suffered untold horrors. Six million of them were put to death—more than half of the population of Canada—and the remnant that has been saved from Hitler's slaughter-house finds neither haven nor peace in Europe today. Their families are dead, their properties destroyed or disposed of, often legally to people who don't want to give it up. In other words, they are excluded socially and economically from Europe which was their home. The Jews of Germany and Poland have passed through bondage infinitely worse than they knew in the land of Egypt. It becomes a question of humanity that we render them all the aid in our power.

While I do not condone terrorism, I do condemn heartily a policy which makes violence inevitable. For thirty years, from the Balfour declaration to the Anglo-American Committee's report, the pledge of Palestine as a Jewish haven has been reiterated. That pledge must be fulfilled. Justice asks it and humanity demands it. The Jews of Europe who were always Britain's friends, are today in concentration camps, while Britain's arch enemy, the Mufti of Jerusalem, goes free to do his mischief. Moshe Shertok [Sharett],[13] the man who raised 25,000 fighting soldiers in Palestine, is now behind barbed wire. The Jews of Europe who suffered so grievously cannot go back to a land of barbed wire and pogroms. They have always been a freedom loving people. They must be given again the opportunity to live again free lives.[14]

Zacks, a prominent Jewish spokesman, reiterated some of Croll's arguments:

Now, fourteen months after the cessation of hostilities in Europe, more than 100,000 displaced Jews live unwanted behind barbed wire in camps administered by Allied Military Governments. In addition, many times that number merely exist from day to day among the 6,000,000 graves in that Europe where Hitler's legions have been vanquished, but where his spirit lives on.[15]

All together, the spokesmen gave an impassioned and detailed presentation of the Jewish position and sought a statement from the Canadian government in support of the recommendation of the Anglo-American Committee of Enquiry that 100,000 Jews be admitted to Palestine.

Unfortunately, the initiative on this issue had been taken by Mackenzie King in a statement to the House of Commons a few days before, when he announced, "I do not believe that any useful purpose would be served by a statement on the situation in Palestine by the Canadian government at the present time."[16]

In the spring of 1947, the whole issue of Palestine's future was turned over to the United Nations. It was proposed that an international committee be appointed to review the problem. The great powers with economic or strategic interests in the Middle East as well as the Arab countries were to be excluded. The committee was therefore made up of eleven small and middle powers, including Canada, in the hope of arriving at a dispassionate solution. The committee was to be known as the UN Special Committee on Palestine (UNSCOP). Initially, Vincent Massey, former Canadian high commissioner in London, was to be the Canadian representative, but when Croll heard of this plan he raised a storm of protest both inside and outside caucus. As a result, the Canadian appointee was Mr. Justice Ivan C. Rand of the Supreme Court of Canada, a happy choice. In the end, the majority report of UNSCOP recommended partition, despite every indication that this would lead to war between the Arabs and the Jews.

On 26 February 1948, Croll spoke before the House of Commons on the Palestine issue. He referred glowingly to Rand's contribution to the UNSCOP report: "The work of Mr. Justice Rand and the members of the Canadian delegation to Lake Success has given Canada a new and impressive position in international affairs and has permitted her to make a notable contribution to world peace."[17] J. L. Ilsley, minister of justice (1946–48), explained Canadian support for partition to the House of Commons: "We are satisfied that, full of difficulties as the partition solution is, any other solution would be worse."[18] The General Assembly had voted in favour of the UNSCOP recommendation on 29 November 1947, an occasion that was joyfully celebrated by Jews all over the world.

In the Commons, Croll was explicit about the urgent need of the Jews for arms:

> The Jews in Palestine are not being reinforced by arms or men from outside. None the less, scarred by the heat that burned six million of their fellowmen, they are determined to fight with whatever arms they have. The Jews today are left without means to defend themselves. They are not permitted to import arms; they are not permitted to import people to fight; they are not permitted to organize an army from their own resources. [19]

Croll failed to mention the covert operations of Haganah, the underground military arm of the Jewish Agency, and the smuggling of both men and arms, but that is understandable. With considerable pride, he referred to the accomplishments of the Jews:

> The Jewish people have initiated the rebirth of human and spiritual values in Palestine. They have developed the economy of the country, established industries and reclaimed land which had lain barren for centuries. [20]

He contended that there was an opportunity for Canada to act as the conscience of the UN in the interests of peace and to pave the way for English-speaking nations to co-operate in implementing the UN decision on partition. The *Canadian Jewish Chronicle* welcomed Croll's speech with superlatives:

> It was altogether a masterly address, and it is most gratifying to Canadian Jewry to realize that it has in the House of Commons a representative who can and will and does, with logic and dignity, bring to expression truths which are so vital to its cause and the cause of justice. [21]

When the new state of Israel was proclaimed, a crowd of twenty thousand gathered in Toronto's Maple Leaf Gardens on Sunday, 16 May 1948, to celebrate. According to the *Toronto Daily Star*:

> A very special storm of applause greeted Lieut. Col. David A. Croll, M.P., when he rose to say that, as a Canadian and a Jew, he was proud to hail the birth of our nation "and to laud the part Canada had played in bringing it to life."

> "Let us not forget that it was Canadian statesmanship that made the UN decision," he said. . . .

> "I am confident that Canada will crown all her efforts on our behalf by granting recognition without delay," he continued, "and that the nations of the world will follow this example. But let us remember that declarations don't make a nation."

> "Every Jew in the world must rededicate himself to build and protect a strong and abiding nation," he said. Jewish veterans of the war not only showed that they could fight but "they have a trained army that stands alone in the Middle East as an efficient, unified force.". . .

> "The past is dead. Let the bitterness and disappointments die with it. For the future we must hold out the hand of friendship toward all."[22]

Croll made his first visit to the new state of Israel in September 1948, as a diversionary manoeuvre. But he put his time to good use spending a few days in Haifa, Tel Aviv and Jerusalem, among other places. He met a number of prominent Israelis during his stay, including David Ben-Gurion, to whose home he was invited. He also renewed his acquaintance with Moshe Sharett, then foreign minister, who was to be his friend for years. Numerous other senior officials, both civilian and military, were glad enough to entertain and inform a member of the Canadian House of Commons who was also a vigorous spokesman for their cause.

Early in December, he reported to the Canadian Club in Ottawa on some of his impressions: "All Israel wants is a chance to settle down and bring peace and western civilization to its little corner of the world—a corner that is smaller than most Ontario counties." He was optimistic about the Israelis:

They have high hopes; they know what they want. They are men and women with determination in their hearts and fire in their bellies. The Jews have returned to the promised land— they have come home—they mean to make the most of it.[23]

Despite the intense lobbying of Croll, Senator Roebuck and others of like mind, Canada did not accord Israel de facto recognition until Christmas Eve 1948. When it was finally announced, however, the Canadian decision was widely acclaimed. Sir Ellsworth Flavelle, chairman of the World Committee for Palestine and the Canadian Palestine Committee, termed it an action for peace "on the highest diplomatic level."[24] When the General Assembly voted on 11 May 1949, to admit Israel, the Canadian vote was affirmative. This action constituted de jure recognition, another moment of triumph for Croll and his Zionist associates.

With official Canadian recognition of the state of Israel, the Israelis at last were able to approach the Canadian government directly to request authorization to buy munitions in Canada, as opposed to earlier clandestine methods. During the early 1950s, Shimon Peres, who was a protégé of David Ben-Gurion and who had worked earlier with Levi Eshkol in

Haganah, was dispatched to Ottawa for this purpose. He was a relatively young man at the time, having been born in Poland in 1923. He records his experience in a long interview with Joëlle Jonathan published in French as *La Force de vaincre* (Jonathan's one interjection in this excerpt is italicized):

In 1952, I left on a mission to Canada to try to purchase munitions. I was trying to obtain some 25-pounder guns and machine guns for Israel. The director general of the Ministry of Defence, Pinhas Sapir, was not in favour of this trip; he thought that I had every chance of failing, and he believed that it would be better to deal through Count Tchernovsky, who claimed to have good contacts in Canada. I had pointed out to him, to no avail, that Tchernovsky was expensive, that he charged a commission of 10 per cent on every deal, and that, all things considered, I felt I could achieve the same result that he could. But Sapir wanted to hear no more. He didn't trust me, and he decided to send Tchernovsky to Canada. Tchernovsky stayed there several weeks without being able to extract the slightest promise from the Canadian government. I then took things into my own hands and left for Canada. Since I knew no-one there, I decided to get in touch with a Canadian member of Parliament, a Jew, Mr. Croll, who had connections with a fellow named McNaughton, the son of the general who had commanded the Canadian armed forces. Through acquaintances, I soon learned that the cabinet was meeting to consider our request. The cabinet's answer was clear: Canada, which refused to sell us offensive arms, was quite willing to supply us with defensive weapons, and agreed to the delivery of the 25-pounders.

But the 25-pounder guns are offensive weapons.

That is true, but most of the members of the Canadian cabinet had fought in the First World War, and at that time 25-

pounder guns did not exist, so they continued to consider the guns to be defensive weapons!

Although I had not got the government to agree to supply the machine guns, I had nevertheless succeeded in part. In part only, because Canada was selling the 25-pounder guns very dear: they were asking $2 million. Sapir, partly surprised and partly jealous of my success, informed me that Israel could not afford to pay such an exorbitant price. It was up to me to find the necessary money myself. I had learned that there was in Canada one of the largest Jewish fortunes in the world, even larger than the Rothschilds'. Bronfman, president of the Canadian Jewish Congress, was one of the largest producers of whisky, and I thought in my innocence that perhaps he could help me. Everyone had tried to dissuade me. Bronfman had the reputation of being stingy, and his associates had bet that he wouldn't give me a penny. Nevertheless, I resolved to meet him. One morning I went directly to his office in the heart of Montreal. [Peres neglects to mention that Croll telephoned Bronfman and arranged the meeting in Montreal.] I explained to the guard at the entrance that I came from Israel and that I absolutely had to speak with Mr. Bronfman. A few minutes later, I was told that he was waiting for me in his office. He was a small man who stared at people attentively during conversations. He told me later that he had an inquisitive nature. Before I started with my request, he wanted to know who had helped me so far in Canada. I naturally gave him Croll's name. He didn't like Croll; he considered him to be unreliable. I later learned that he had disapproved of his attitude in the past in one specific instance, and that he had borne a bit of a grudge against him ever since. I gave him all the facts of the case, and explained that the Canadian government had agreed to sell us the guns but the price they wanted was too high. He himself realized that $2 million was too much to ask for second-hand guns. Bronfman was a man of action; he greatly admired Napoleon, whose battles he had at his finger-tips. My approach pleased him, and he agreed right away to help me. He got up from his armchair and said to me, "let's go to Ottawa right away". I couldn't believe my ears. Bronfman stopped for a moment, his eyes fixed on the bottom of my trousers, and murmured, "Your *kibbutznik* socks are too light-coloured... you will have to get a darker pair before we go...." I was prepared to change the colour of my socks in order to get the guns! We left for Ottawa in his Cadillac. In the course of the trip, he stopped for a drink of good well-aged Scotch. I had never before in my life tasted whisky, but I couldn't decently refuse to keep him company, so I had to swallow a large glass of it. The minster of trade and commerce, Mr. Howe, was at that time one of the most influential men in the Canadian government. We had barely arrived in Ottawa when Bronfman phoned him. A few minutes later Howe received us in his department. Bronfman was a direct man. He explained our situation concisely: "Israel needs guns. Canada is able to sell them. The guns which have piled up in army surplus will be extremely valuable to Israel. Your cabinet has agreed, and you have asked $2 million. Two million dollars is too much; you ought to agree to sell them for $1 million." I was amazed at his audacity. The minister, who was probably familiar with his manner, reflected for a moment and promised to look into the matter. This was not good enough for Bronfman. "We can't wait," he said. "We need an answer right away." Howe immediately called the deputy minister and the minister of defense. Canada agreed to sell us the guns for $1 1/2 million. We had saved half a million dollars. Bronfman was pleased. I was both pleased and worried, since we didn't even have $1 1/2 million. Bronfman didn't know that, and after all that he had done for us, I didn't dare tell him. I was so afraid of upsetting him and spoiling his pleasure that I waited a little before telling him. I was so ill at ease and so awkward, I recall, that he noticed it. I blurted out my words, as though to get it over with as quickly as possible: "I forgot to mention that we don't have the $1 1/2 million, and I hope that you can help us find it." What a surprise! He was taken with this new idea, and we returned to Montreal at once. He already had a plan for the next day. "Shimon," he said, "now you must buy a dark suit with black socks. You must be smartly dressed; tomorrow night, I am going to have a large party at my home. I am going to invite all the Jewish community." He lived in a great mansion on a hill. There was about thirty guests, I believe, and we had an extremely fine dinner. His wife was charming, and she immediately took a liking to me. In the course of the evening, Bronfman succeeded in winning the support of all the Jewish community, to such an extent that we were able to collect all the money that was needed. This warm-hearted man had succeeded completely: he had obtained a reduction in the price of the guns, and he had even raised the money to pay for them. I immediately telephoned Israel to report the two pieces of news. No-one would believe me. Sapir treated me as if I were bluffing. Several months later, Israel received the first shipment of guns."[25]

There is some truth in Peres's statement that Bronfman was not one of Croll's admirers. When Croll was preparing to run in Spadina in 1945, his financial position was poor. Bronfman generously offered to pay the total cost of Croll's campaign, but Croll rejected his offer, considering it unwise to be so completely obligated to one man. Understandably, Bronfman was displeased, with the upshot that he gave Croll nothing.

It is also true that Croll was intimately associated with A. R. L. "Andy" McNaughton in the procurement of munitions for the Haganah and later Israel. McNaughton, a Canadian RCAF veteran, and the son of Gen. A. G. L. McNaughton, appears to have started exporting war surplus from Canada to Palestine in 1946. He dealt extensively with the Canadian War Assets Corporation, and when he was in need of legal advice or assistance with the Ottawa bureaucracy, it was perhaps only natural that he should turn to Croll. Croll, who became his close friend, also assisted him in obtaining appointment as an official agent of the Israeli government. McNaughton's activities impinged upon the Ottawa empire of C. D. Howe, who, as minister of reconstruction and supply, was naturally privy to all surplus disposal questions and knew that Croll, from time to time, exerted pressure to expedite the sale of surplus munitions destined by whatever indirection for the Jewish armed forces. In some quarters, there was a definite feeling that Croll overstepped the bounds of acceptable behaviour for a member of Parliament. Croll was careful to avoid anything illegal and stayed well in the background, but he used his influence even when doing so was in conflict with cabinet policy. Croll was incapable of turning away from the anguished appeals of the Yishuv (the Jewish settlement in Palestine before 1948), even though he knew that answering them might cause problems for him.

The government of Israel, of course, had other reasons as well to be grateful to Croll. For one thing, he had been generous in his personal contributions to the young country, and for another, he had been instrumental in fund raising on a large scale. His main contribution, however, was his aggressive intervention with the Canadian government on behalf of Israeli interests. In the fall of 1952, Joseph Gottlieb, executive director of the Jewish National Fund, paid him tribute:

The Jewish National Fund and the people of Israel owe a debt to him for his inspired and untiring efforts to aid the state of Israel and to bring about a better understanding between both countries.[26]

One way the Israelis showed their esteem was to name a piece of desert after him. An area of 500 *dunams* (about 125 acres) in the Negev was to be designated Nahlat David Croll. *Nahlat* can be translated as "estate." Croll was presented with a scroll describing this honour by Samuel Ussishkin of the General Zionist Party of Israel at the annual Negev dinner of the Jewish National Fund at the Royal York Hotel in Toronto early in December 1952. The 750 guests at the dinner donated $35,000 to the reclamation of this land. Croll said in reply, "I regard myself merely as a symbol of those Jews who have added to their responsibilities as Canadians the additional burden of assisting the rebuilding of their spiritual homeland."[27]

The government of Israel wanted to present Croll with a medal as an indication of their gratitude. Canada's external affairs minister, L. B. Pearson, recommended against acceptance, however, evidently feeling that it might confirm fears in some quarters that Croll had a dual loyalty. Croll agreed. Pearson and Croll had fairly frequent and generally useful exchanges of views on the Middle East. They were also friends. Roughly the same age, they shared an interest in sports, especially baseball, and tried to outdo one another with tales of their boyhood heroes. Above all, they were both passionately concerned about the fate of Jews in the postwar world.

Croll made his second trip to Israel later in 1955, after he had been elevated to the Senate. By this time, he was well and favourably known to the Israeli authorities. Pearson suggested he call on the United States ambassador to Israel, Edward B. Lawson, to persuade him to urge the Israelis to offer compensation to the Arabs for land taken by force. Pearson's view was that ultimately any money required would be forthcoming from the United States. Croll did make the call, but nothing ever came of it.

For David Croll and many like him, Israel is a cultural fulfillment, a home for the heart of the no longer eternally wandering Jew. Of course Israel has a profound religious significance as well, and no one felt this more keenly than David's father, Hillel Croll. Hillel was mildly impressed that his son knew Shimon Peres and Teddy Kollek and that he had been invited to David Ben-Gurion's house. But when he was invited to dine at the home of the Chief Rabbi of Jerusalem, that was an epic event.

Once during Croll's 1955 visit, the Israeli military organized a grand cocktail party in Croll's honour. At the last minute, someone checking the details discovered that they had no rye whisky. Unwilling to chance offending their guest, they dispatched an aircraft to Cyprus for a supply of Canadian Club. Despite its importance to the economy of Windsor-Walkerville, Croll had a lifelong distaste for this particular beverage. He was nevertheless obliged, rye in hand, to fulfill his hosts' image of a Canadian.

Croll continues to this day to dedicate himself to Jewish causes, but strict orthodoxy has little appeal for him, and he has privately criticized some of the ultra-orthodox doctrines imposed in Israel. He has been an adherent of conservative Judaism for many years and belongs to the Beth Tzedec congregation in Toronto, one of the largest in the world. He also joined the Holy Blossom Temple, a reform congregation, not for doctrinal reasons but because of its excellent scholastic facilities. His attendance at the synagogue is irregular, in contrast to his father's, but he always appears on High Holy Days and on other special occasions. He does, however, follow his father's example as a faithful visitor of the sick. He is often to be found early in the morning bustling about one of the Toronto hospitals to see some ailing friend or other. After Arthur Roebuck, his kindred spirit in politics for so many years, suffered an incapacitating stroke and was confined first to the hospital and then to a nursing home, Croll regularly visited him once a week, despite the fact that Roebuck was no longer able to recognize him.

Since its inception, Croll has been a member of the Jewish War Veterans of Canada, a body with aims similar to those of the Royal Canadian Legion. There are branches or posts of the Jewish War Veterans in most major Canadian cities. At its general convention in October 1979, Croll was named national commander, a position he was to hold for over ten years. In July 1980, he was also named president of the Jewish War Veterans Community and Charity Trust, the objective of which is to provide funds for humanitarian, welfare, educational and religious purposes for Jewish war veterans and their families. Indeed, in 1982, he undertook a personal fund raising campaign for the Trust. In his capacity as national commander, Croll, among his other duties, represented the Jewish War Veterans of Canada at the annual Remembrance Day services, where, thanks to his efforts, rabbis have taken their place alongside Christian priests and clergymen.

Croll also belongs to the Canadian Council of Christians and Jews, which was founded in 1947. As its name implies, the purpose of this organization is to promote greater harmony and understanding between Jews and Christians, although in recent years it has also concerned itself with racial discrimination of all types. It is "an association of men and women who seek by educational means to promote justice, friendship, cooperation and understanding among people differing in race, religion or nationality." He was elected one of the directors of the council in 1953, has served as a member of the executive committee since about 1960 and is a recipient of the council's Human Relations Award.

NINE

Making the Best of It

AN APPOINTMENT TO THE CANADIAN SENATE MAY NO longer be looked upon as one of the glittering prizes of life, but there was a time when the promise of Senate seat, expressed or intimated, could call forth the most valiant of political efforts or loosen the tightest of purse strings. The issue of rewarding the generosity of faithful party donors, however, appears to have been especially complex and protracted when the individuals in question happened to be Jews. Various hopefuls aspired from the early 1920s onwards. Promises were made, but thirty years later, none had been kept.

During the early 1950s, it was natural that Prime Minister St. Laurent should seek Croll's counsel on the appointment of a Jewish senator. Croll had two suggestions to offer. The first was Lazarus Phillips, a scholarly lawyer from Montreal who was closely associated with Sam Bronfman. The second was Sam Godfrey, a prominent Toronto businessman.

The most persistent contender after 1945, however, was Sam Bronfman of the Distillers Corporation-Seagram's Limited of Montreal. Bronfman had made substantial contributions to the Liberal party over the years and felt entitled to the recognition. Appointment as Canada's first Jewish senator would remove any stigma lingering from the dark days when Bronfman was involved in the liquor-running business in Saskatchewan and elsewhere. But the past was not easily forgiven or forgotten. For example, M. J. Coldwell, the highly respected leader of the CCF, once publicly criticized the mere invitation of Bronfman to a state dinner at Government House. Another difficulty was that J. G. Gardiner, the Liberal minister of agriculture (1935–57) and former premier of Saskatchewan, was very much aware that any favour for Sam Bronfman would not be popular in western Canada. Gardiner's influence on the question was important. But all the lobbying one way or another foundered on the rock of C. D. Howe, upon whose judgement St. Laurent relied heavily. Howe decisively rejected Bronfman.

In the late spring of 1955, when Croll was summoned to the prime minister's office, he expected that finally he was to be named to the cabinet. Instead, St. Laurent informed him that anti-Semitism in the party and in Quebec was sufficiently strong to preclude this possibility. St. Laurent made it clear that whereas he had no sympathy for this sentiment, he did not consider it politically realistic to ignore such deep-seated attitudes. Croll was deeply hurt. Like many others, he had had great respect for Louis St. Laurent. He had admired the quality of St. Laurent's mind and his apparent sense of fairness, even though he believed that the prime minister's political talents were limited and at times gave the impression that Quebec, not Canada, was his primary concern. Now, with Croll's hopes of cabinet appointment shattered by the barriers of ignorance and bigotry, the years he had spent trying to eradicate racial and religious intolerance seemed misspent. As a consolation, St. Laurent offered to make him a senator. Croll politely refused.

By the mid-1950s, the government found itself under increasing pressure both to appoint a Jewish senator and to accord Toronto appropriate recognition in the cabinet. Since St. Laurent was unwilling to appoint Croll to the cabinet, and since he did not dare appoint anyone else from Toronto over Croll's head, Croll's elevation to the Senate became urgent. When St. Laurent next approached Croll in the summer of 1955, his message was conveyed by a trusted emissary, the minister of finance, Walter Harris, also a friend of Croll's. Harris told Croll that if he persisted in his refusal to go to the Senate, it would be a long time before another Jew was considered. The government would be in a position to say to the Jewish community that the offer had been made but rejected.

Croll agonized over his decision for nearly a week. He consulted family, friends and political associates. There was no consensus in the advice he received. He felt that he had come to the end of his political career and was distraught. Many years later, his wife intimated that she would not care to live through another week of such misery. Croll's dilemma was not entirely personal, since any decision he made would affect many others. The dominant factor in his decision was the responsibility he felt to Canadian Jewry. Finally, and with great reluctance, he agreed with as much grace as he could muster.

Author Peter Newman recounts that

> Sam Bronfman and a caucus of his senior executives were conferring in Seagram's boardroom on the morning of 28 July 1955 when Robina Shanks, his secretary, brought in the bad news [about Croll's Senate appointment]. Max Henderson, who was there, remembers Sam exploding, parading about the room in a kind of military mourner's slow march, wailing, "I'm the king of the Jews! It should have been mine. . . . I bought it! I paid for it! Those treacherous bastards did me in!"[1]

According to Max Henderson, secretary-treasurer of Distillers Corporation-Seagram's at the time, one of the reasons for Bronfman's chagrin was that he had told some of his friends in the United States that he expected to be appointed.[2] His bitterness was not diminished when his friend and counsellor, Lazarus Phillips, finally was named to the Senate by Prime Minister Pearson on Croll's advice in 1968. When St. Laurent announced Croll's appointment, he said that although the new Senator was being named a Toronto representative, "I expect that he will be looked upon as a representative of fellow-Canadians of Jewish origin throughout the country."[3]

There were many who wished Croll well, among them the *Globe and Mail*:

> Mr. David Croll also brings long experience to the Senate, having spent the last quarter-century in municipal, Provincial and Federal politics. This newspaper has always been impressed by Mr. Croll's considerable abilities, and has long wondered why they got so little recognition from his party. In the Senate, we trust, he will be appreciated as he deserves to be.[4]

When a by-election was called in Spadina in the fall of 1955, the *Globe and Mail* continued its unrelenting attack on the St. Laurent government's treatment of Croll:

> The reason for the by-election, which is the appointment of Mr. David Croll to the Senate, is in itself an issue or should be. A senatorship is one of the pleasantest things that can happen to an average politician in Canada. Mr. Croll, who sat for Spadina from 1945 until this year, is not an average politician but a man of exceptional brains, experience and generosity of spirit. Kicking him upstairs was not the way to recognize his services or use his talents.

> Mr. Croll should have been appointed to the Cabinet. The Prime Minister promised this part of the country representa-

tion in his Ministry; and Mr. Croll was easily the ablest Liberal MP available. It was to avoid making him a Minister that Mr. St. Laurent shelved him in the Senate. Spadina voters may well take next Monday's opportunity to censure the Government for this brazen bit of opportunism and intolerance.[5]

Whether or not Croll's appointment was an issue in the minds of the voters in Spadina, Charles E. Rea emerged victorious for the Progressive Conservatives over Liberal Sam Godfrey.

Although Croll was appointed to the Senate on 28 July 1955, Parliament did not reconvene until 10 January 1956. As usual, the opening ceremonies were both colourful and impressive. Whereas he continued to have private misgivings, Croll had reason to be pleased about one thing. His mother and his wife were present on the floor of the Senate when he was escorted into the chamber. It was a proud moment for Minka and Sarah Croll. Unfortunately, Hillel had been gathered to his fathers several months before and could not see this latest achievement of his oldest son's.

When Croll gave his maiden speech in the Senate on 18 January 1956, an unaccustomed number of reporters and observers gathered in the galleries. He was a seconder of the Address in Reply to the Speech from the Throne and ranged widely in his comments. In some of Croll's initial interviews with the press after his appointment to the Senate, he said frankly that he had been propelled and not gently led by the hand to his reward. By now, however, he had had several months to reflect and was more diplomatic in his speech, saying that the Senate was not a sanctuary and should not be regarded as an escape from responsibility and service.[6]

One of Croll's observations about the Senate as an investigative body is of particular interest, since it anticipated the role he was to play with distinction for many years:

It has always been my view and this is the first opportunity I have had to say it, that the Senate can play a very much more important role than it does in the field of public inquiry. . . . If there is wisdom among us, and I believe there is, and if there is experience of many years, as I am sure there is, then these qualities should be put to use in the most beneficial manner. Frankly, the Senate of Canada faces the task of reviving public confidence in it. I know of no better way of accomplishing that end than by continuing to use our talent and experience in the undivided service of our people in the field of public inquiry.[7]

Croll's conviction that the Senate could perform useful work as an investigative body had a long history. In 1934, when he moved to Toronto as a member of Hepburn's cabinet, he brought with him as an administrative assistant Dave Connery, a friend who had been city editor of the *Windsor Star* and a well-known news broadcaster. Connery had a special talent for public relations, and before long, he was induced to return to private industry in Detroit. He later joined the staff of Senator Patrick V. McNamara of Michigan as executive assistant. Croll and Connery kept in touch, and in their many discussions, Connery described in detail the operation of the U.S. Senate committees and their investigative role. Croll became convinced of the validity of the American experience and in due course was able to persuade W. Ross Macdonald, then government leader in the Senate, to his point of view. In turn, Macdonald convinced John T. Haig, his Conservative counterpart, that the use of Senate committees as investigative tools was valid and likely to be fruitful.[8]

Throughout his many years in the Senate, Croll has served at one time or another on nearly all the standing committees and many of its special committees. The work done in the committees has been the most important function of the Canadian Senate, and Croll contributed regularly, although there were occasions when his heart was not in it. For example, one of his first assignments was to serve on the Standing Committee on Divorce. At the time, the Senate acted as divorce court for Quebec and Newfoundland, since the power of the provincial courts to deal with divorce was limited or did not exist in those provinces. Years later, in 1968, Croll confessed on the floor of the Senate that he was not happy with his role:

> When I came into the Senate some 13 years ago I was dragged into the Standing Committee on Divorce. I did everything I could to avoid it, but I was told that they needed some lawyers and that they had contested cases and it was my duty to be there. Well, I was the best saboteur they ever put on the committee because from the day I got there I urged that they get out of this business. We had no right to deal with matters of divorce. I did not think it was dignified or a matter the Senate should be concerned with, and I did everything I could to hasten its removal from the Senate.[9]

On the positive side, it was the development of the Senate's investigative functions, especially after the defeat of the Diefenbaker government in 1963, that allowed Croll to pursue unabated his interest in advancing the cause of disadvantaged groups in Canada. For example, although he had been instrumental in pushing the Liberal party to adopt significant reforms in the administration of old age pensions, he was convinced that much remained to be done to improve the lot of old people in our society. Thus, in July 1963, he proposed the establishment of the Special Senate Committee on Aging, the purpose of which was to examine the problems involved in the promotion of the welfare of the aged and aging persons, in order to ensure that in addition to the provision of sufficient income, there are also developed adequate services and facilities of a positive and preventive kind so that older persons may continue to live healthy and useful lives as members of the Canadian community and the need for the maximum co-operation of all levels of governments in the promotion thereof. . . . [10]

The underlying aims of the committee, as described by Croll, who became its chairman, were ambitious. They were to examine the whole problem of aging persons in Canada, including health, income, employment, leisure, housing, care and assistance. The facts about these aspects of aging in Canada, the United States, the United Kingdom and the Scandinavian countries were to be established. Then methods of improving the current situation in Canada were to be recommended. Croll was able to forecast accurately what the future held:

> The second half of this century will be terminated with an increasing number of older people, and medical science tells' us that the life expectancy will rise even above the present 71 years, so that the proportion of senior citizens to the rest of the population will continue to increase. [11]

The committee began its hearings in October 1963 and held thirty-two meetings, which continued until December 1964. The witnesses included spokesmen for three provincial and thirty-six municipal governments, sixty national organizations and thirteen individuals with special expertise in the field of aging. The churches were well represented, as were a wide assortment of social agencies, such as the Montreal

Council of Social Agencies, the Social Planning Council of Metropolitan Toronto, the Ottawa Welfare Council and the Canadian Association of Social Workers. Various witnesses from the medical profession appeared on behalf of such organizations as the American Geriatrics Society, the Canadian Mental Health Association, the Canadian Medical Association and the Allen Memorial Institute of Psychiatry of McGill University. There were a number of representatives of nursing homes, as well as the Victorian Order of Nurses. Such veteran witnesses as the Canadian Chamber of Commerce, the Canadian Federation of Agriculture and the Canadian Labour Congress testified. In addition, there were scores of written briefs.

The testimony brought out clearly some of the changes that had occurred in Canada. In a traditional society, the elderly were regarded highly. In the agricultural sector, for example, these were still the people who knew from long observation and experience how best to contend with the vagaries of weather and the sundry problems of field and animal husbandry. But in a modern industrial society, change had become so rapid that older people were often overcome by the pace of electronic wizardry, the technical aspects of new gadgetry based on microcomputers and lasers often remaining a mystery to them. This was a problem that became particularly serious when such advances in the workplace left employees near retirement age with the feeling that their status had been impaired.

There were a number of interesting observations about the once-common pattern of three generations living under one roof. Older people, it now seemed, liked to be near their married children but no longer wished to live with them. The crowding of too many generations under one inadequate roof led to hostility and unhappiness. Excessive dependence of the elderly on relatives was to be avoided. And if their independence was interrupted because of illness or other disability, careful attention needed to be paid to rehabilitation.

The testimony of many witnesses attested that a significant percentage of old people were poor. They could not maintain the standard of living to which they were accustomed before retirement because their personal finances were gradually being eroded by inflation. The question of an adequate income was dealt with often and at length and, as might be expected, with considerable variation in views. To recommend someone else's standard of living is not an easy exercise for mere mortals. The other difficulty was that any prescribed level rapidly became obsolete in a time of social and economic change.

The hearings of the Special Senate Committee on Aging were completed in December 1964 and its final report finished in September 1965. However, it was not tabled in the Senate until 2 February 1966. The end product was a medium-sized book of nearly two hundred pages. Croll was proud of this report and referred to it as "bold, brave and imaginative." He stressed the urgency of the needs of old people, saying, "The old cannot wait; what they need, they need now."

The report contained ninety-two recommendations, but despite Croll's brash claim that they were all important, the first recommendation was the most significant. Croll summarized it in his statement on the floor of the Senate:

> We recommend that the Government guarantee a minimum income as of right to all persons 65 years of age who have resided in Canada for ten years, without a means test or a needs test, of $1,260 for a single person and $2,220 for a married couple; that the Government should pay the difference between these levels and the actual income, this to be adjusted annually on the basis of consumers' price indices. [12]

He emphasized that these were established figures, being the maximum income permitted under the Old Age Assistance Act. This act was designed to supplement the incomes of those between the ages of sixty-five and sixty-nine before they became eligible for Old Age Security pensions at seventy. The means test applicable at the time meant that an income of less than $1,260 per annum for a single person and $2,220 for a married couple would qualify them for supplementary income.

Some years later, Croll referred to the consequences of his committee's recommendations:

> In the course of our recommendations, of which there were 92, we came up with a blockbuster, for the first recommendation we made in our report was to reduce the age for Old Age Security from 70 to 65 and to provide a basic income. The government accepted it within a very short time.[13]

One of the fundamental conclusions of the Committee, buttressed by statistical evidence and expert witnesses, was that older people, in general, make up a low-income group. Specific action was required to increase the benefits paid to those seventy and over so that at least their incomes would move up with those of the general population. The reintroduction of a means test to justify the increase in the level of the old age pension was categorically rejected. To increase the old age pension by itself was not sufficient, since the prospective introduction of the Canada/Quebec Pension Plan would lead to inequities in the treatment of different strata among the elderly. The committee decided that the answer was to establish an income-guarantee program such that everyone over sixty-five would have a right to a minimum annual income at levels set out in the Old Age Assistance Act.

Employment opportunities for the elderly are of course heavily influenced by employment levels throughout the economy. Nevertheless, the committee urged a change in attitude towards older workers, noting that for certain classes of work, older employees had highly desirable qualities, such as reliability, good judgement and low absenteeism. The committee made a number of recommendations to reduce discrimination against older workers and to encourage more vocational training and opportunities for part-time work for older people.

Impressed by the testimony of the Canadian Medical Association, the Department of National Health and Welfare and various private organizations about the importance of health care for the elderly, the committee therefore proposed that geriatric clinics be established and that a major effort be made to provide health counselling by local community organizations. It also stressed the importance of home health care under local direction, lamented the lack of facilities for the care of long-term patients and proposed the construction of additional institutional facilities to deal with both mental and physical illness. It recognized the importance of nursing homes and stressed the importance of proper standards and supervision.

Under the general heading of community services, the committee urged the establishment of programs to integrate the lives of older people into the community. These ranged from homemaker services for shut-ins to centres sponsored by churches, libraries, schools and so on, which would carry out activities specifically designed to meet the needs of old people. Generally, the committee suggested that health care professionals should pay greater attention to geriatric medicine. Finally, it recommended the creation of a national commission on aging designed to provide leadership in areas of concern to the elderly and to keep their problems under review.

As Croll wrote in his foreword to the final report, its analysis was the first attempt "to examine the problems of aged Canadians as a whole on a national scale."[14] Whereas there is little doubt that the committee made a significant contribution to the understanding of many aspects of the problems of aging, its single greatest achievement came in 1967, when the government introduced legislation providing for a guaranteed income supplement to those receiving the Old Age Security pension, provided that need existed. The amount of the Guaranteed Income Supplement did not precisely match the levels proposed by the committee, but the principle was established. The Old Age Security pension and the Guaranteed Income Supplement remain the cornerstones of federal social welfare policy in dealing with poverty among the aging.[15]

For his role as a chairman of the Special Senate Committee on Aging, Croll was recognized by the American Geriatrics Society with an honorary membership at its meeting in Toronto in May 1970. It was a distinction indeed because this body of medical professionals rarely designates laymen as honorary members.

TEN

The Heyday of the Consumer

EARLY IN 1960, SENATOR PAUL DOUGLAS INTRODUCED A bill in the United States Senate calling for the disclosure of the cost of credit transactions. This "truth in lending" bill required that borrowing costs be stated as an absolute amount and that the equivalent effective annual rate of interest be expressed as a percentage.

On 16 March 1960, Croll introduced a private members' bill in the Senate (S-25), which came to be known as the Finance Charges (Disclosure) Bill, with similar aims. He explained its purpose briefly:

> This bill requires the disclosure of interest rates and finance charges when credit is extended, so that the borrower or instalment buyer will know exactly what rate of annual interest he is charged for a loan or purchase and what his total cost will be.[1]

At the time of second reading on 11 May, Croll expanded on the objects of his bill. He stated that misleading and deceptive methods were often used to show the cost of credit. Borrowers had to have sufficient knowledge of credit alternatives and

their associated costs before the benefits of effective competi-
tion could be achieved. He also suggested that individuals
might be accumulating excessive debt because of their inability to assess its costs.[2]

Those senators who believed their primary function was to
protect and advance the well-being of Canada's financial
institutions—and there were a fair number who did—were
quick to respond. Senator Salter Hayden, senior partner in
the prestigious Toronto law firm of McCarthy and McCarthy,
director of the Bank of Nova Scotia and chairman of the
Standing Senate Committee on Banking and Commerce,
gave a long and carefully crafted rebuttal of Croll's arguments.
Two points, to be repeated ad nauseam by the finance companies and their representatives, were summarized by Hayden:

> The problems posed in trying to translate borrowing costs into
> terms of simple interest are very difficult. I feel very strongly
> that if the borrower is told the cost in dollars he has enough
> information.[3]

He also stated that Croll's bill was not constitutionally sound.
Nevertheless, on 23 June, the bill was referred to committee,
where it died when the third session of the Twenty-fourth
Parliament was prorogued.

In Canada, the constitutional aspects of interest and consumer credit are tangled. Parliament is assigned responsibility
for interest, banks and banking, and bills of exchange,
whereas the provincial legislatures are empowered to regulate
consumer credit contracts. The delineation of authority to
deal with consumer credit is therefore far from clear-cut.
However, in the period prior to prorogation on 11 August, detailed consideration had been given to this question. The law
clerk and parliamentary counsel of the Senate had given an
opinion, dated 25 July 1960, that Croll's bill was indeed

within the federal power. Croll consequently resubmitted his bill during the fourth session of Parliament on 14 December 1960.[4] The Senate banking lobby was not prepared to allow another round of committee hearings, however, and his motion for second reading was defeated 35–26 on 23 May 1961.[5]

Meanwhile, in the United States, the proposals of Senator Douglas were also encountering stiff opposition. This was at best cold comfort to Croll, especially when his Canadian opponents were able to find ready-made arguments laid out in the hearings of congressional committees and in the *Congressional Record*. But impervious to rebuffs, Croll reintroduced his bill, now known as S-3, on 1 November 1962. This was his third try. On 6 December 1962, he moved second reading, and despite Hayden's expressed opposition, it was referred once more to the Standing Senate Committee on Banking and Commerce.[6] Unfortunately, the dissolution of Parliament prevented further progress. When Croll made a fourth attempt during the short 1962–63 parliamentary session, dissolution again intervened.

Then, on 5 June 1963, Croll rose in the Senate to state:

> This is the fifth occasion on which I have moved the second reading of a bill similar to S-6. I make no apology for my perseverance, although it might appear that I am creating some kind of record as far as this chamber is concerned.[7]

And for the fifth time, Hayden announced his opposition.

In fairness to the opponents of the bill, it should be pointed out that there was litigation stemming from the Ontario Unconscionable Transactions Act before the Supreme Court of Canada. It was anticipated that the judgment would settle the issue of constitutionality. Croll was not a constitutional lawyer, although with a little help from his friends, he was able to hold his own in argument on the floor of the Senate. He simply was not inclined to subside into inaction because of some constitutional bogey. There were important social issues to be dealt with and remedial action was his goal. Whether this required federal or provincial or co-operative action was of secondary importance to him. The issue of jurisdiction was, nevertheless, a matter of substance and one that deserved careful consideration.

The same could not be said for some of the bogus arguments put forward by Croll's opponents. One of these was the claim that there was no single correct way of calculating the appropriate percentage rate. Time and again, the claim was made that the calculations of interest rates were so complex that they would tax the capacity of a professional mathematician.

In the meantime, some grass roots support started to build. The Consumers' Association of Canada, the co-operatives, the credit unions and the trade unions began to take a more aggressive interest in the issue of interest rate disclosure and offer Croll much-needed help. A number of private members' bills were introduced in the House of Commons paralleling Croll's or proposing even more sweeping changes, such as upper limits on all interest rates, or amending various provisions of the Small Loans Act. These bills were a signal to the government that the time had come to give "truth in lending" legislation some serious attention.

Finally in November 1963, a special joint committee of the Senate and the House of Commons on consumer credit was created.[8] Croll was the Senate cochairman and J. J. Greene, M.P. for Renfrew South, the cochairman for the House of Commons until his appointment as minister of agriculture in the Pearson cabinet in December 1965. He was replaced by Ron Basford, a young lawyer, who had first been elected for Vancouver-Burrard in 1963. The committee met nineteen times between June 1964 and April 1966 and provided a valuable forum for the examination of disclosure legislation.

The lenders, including companies licensed under the Small Loans Act, and the sales finance companies were represented by the Canadian Consumer Loan Association and the Federated Council of Sales Finance Companies, respectively. Not unexpectedly, the principal argument of the sales finance companies was that the cost of credit expressed as a dollar amount was far more meaningful to the consumer than disclosure in the form of interest rates. They claimed that the enforced disclosure of rates would be a disservice to the consumer. There was now, however, a succession of sympathetic witnesses to balance the opponents of full disclosure.

The joint committee was not to be alone in its concern with truth in lending. The Royal Commission on Banking and Finance addressed this question in its 1964 report and dismissed the argument that different methods of calculation give different results. It concluded that there was a strong case for the disclosure of both the absolute and the percentage costs of borrowing. In addition, when the Select Committee of the Ontario Legislature on Consumer Credit presented its findings in 1965, it came out strongly in favour of better disclosure rules, as did the 1965 Royal Commission on the Cost of Borrowing Money in Nova Scotia.

The preparation of the report of the joint committee on consumer credit began in July 1966 and was completed in February 1967. Recognizing the constitutional and jurisdictional issues involved and that its recommendations covered both federal and provincial territory, the committee report stated that "if the problem is to be attacked completely, there will be need for the utmost federal provincial co-operation. . . . "[9] In all, the committee made eighteen recommendations, the bulk of which dealt with disclosure and the elimination of shady lending practices. It proposed that the ceiling under the Small Loans Act be increased from $1,500 to $5,000 and also endorsed the principle of legislation to provide relief from unconscionable transactions. It suggested that maximum rates of interest be adopted for financing used cars as well as for other types of consumer credit transactions. In one of its recommendations, it is possible to detect the hand of its Senate cochairman: a proposal to provide government-guaranteed consumer loans up to a maximum of $1,500 to poor families. Such loans were to be repayable over a reasonable period at a low rate of interest, not unlike loans made by the government to countries in the Third World.

By the latter half of 1966, the combined efforts of the royal commissions, the parliamentary committees and the United States congressional hearings were being felt, particularly by the provinces. To ensure uniformity from province to province and to harmonize federal regulations affecting banks and other credit-granting institutions, a federal/provincial conference was held in Ottawa on 19–20 December 1966 with Mitchell Sharp, then minister of finance, as chairman. Nova Scotia, which had progressed further than the other provinces, emphasized the desirability of universality in consumer credit legislation and co-ordinated action by the federal government. In response, Sharp confirmed that new regulations governing the chartered banks would be introduced shortly. Further discussions by federal and provincial officials were held on 4–5 April 1967.

In the meantime, some of the provincial disclosure legislation that had been under consideration became law. The Nova Scotia Consumer Protection Act, 1966, was proclaimed on 15 January 1967, and the corresponding Ontario act went into effect on 31 July 1967. Disclosure legislation has since been passed by all the provinces. On 15 September 1967, the Bank Cost of Borrowing Disclosure Regulations were issued under section 92 of the Bank Act, which set forth the new disclosure rules for the chartered banks. The differences between the federal and the provincial regulations were not substantial.

The provinces may have seized the initiative on enacting truth-in-lending legislation, but the joint committee, and Croll in particular, deserves the lion's share of the credit for publicizing and promoting this important public safeguard. Croll referred to this fact on the floor of the Senate in the fall of 1966: "It is true that this question [disclosure] lies within their provincial jurisdiction, but their [the provinces'] action has been the direct result of what we undertook. . . . "[10]

Although the bulk of the work of the joint committee had been completed by mid-1966, a new set of consumer problems was looming. Considerable public agitation developed over soaring food prices during the spring and summer of 1966. Croll came up with the useful idea of converting this committee into a forum for investigating the vexing question of consumer prices. This was a convenient proposal from the government's point of view because the administrative machinery of the committee was still in place and ready to move quickly. Accordingly, on 8 September 1966, Mitchell Sharp moved an amendment to the committee's terms of reference, instructing it "to also enquire into and report upon the trends in the cost of living in Canada and factors which may have contributed to changes in the cost of living in Canada in recent months."[11] On 13 September, on the motion of the government leader in the Senate, John Connolly, the Senate agreed.[12] Not the least of the advantages of this procedure was that the committee inherited David Croll as Senate cochairman. Connolly observed with a certain wry humour:

I am sure we all have very great confidence in the cochairman (Hon. Mr. Croll) and in the initiative he has shown on other occasions in respect of committee work, the last one being the Committee on Aging. I think we can rely upon his youth as well as his drive to accomplish a great deal through this committee.[13]

In the House of Commons, Opposition leader John Diefenbaker complained with some justification:

Too often the setting up of a committee is nothing but a subterfuge on the part of the government to get away from making any decision or taking any action that has to be taken.[14]

The principal targets of the committee in the fall of 1966 were the major retailers and wholesalers of food, as well as the large manufacturers of processed foods and other household products, such as detergents. Promotional devices such as trading stamps and premiums were also under attack by various consumer groups, and the committee was naturally interested in the effect of such devices on prices.

On the whole, the retail food chains and the major food processors and manufacturers of consumer goods appeared to welcome the opportunity to present their case, and the adversarial aspects of the inquiry were not significant, although some of the questioning by members was querulous at times. At one point, Croll said, "The president of one of the chain stores [Sam Steinberg] said to me, 'This is a wonderful thing to do, Dave—every 30 years!' "[15]

The committee had a hectic schedule of hearings in the fall of 1966 and on 20 December tabled its interim report, which was contained in ten printed pages. Brevity was an advantage because the press and the other media could digest its findings quickly. Consequently, there was wide coverage of the committee's conclusions.

Some of the recommendations of the committee were

couched in general terms, but on the subject of packaging and labelling it became quite specific:

> Facts should be presented in a prominent place on the package or container in a form which is legible and free from graphic distortion. Where applicable, the ingredients should be revealed both by name and percentage of composition, and the consumer should also know about the quality of the product.

> *In particular:*

> (1) the product should be described by its generic name where this is meaningful;
> (2) where products are of a certain type, variety and quality, they should be graded;
> (3) packages should be designed in terms of size, shape or dimension in a way that will not deceive or mislead retail purchasers;
> (4) the net quantity of the contents in terms of weight or measure should be expressed as simply as possible and in terms which can be easily interpreted;
> (5) the essential information about a packaged product and its physical contents should be stated in a prominent place on the label.[16]

On the basis of these suggestions, a new Consumer Packaging and Labelling Act was drawn up and given Royal Assent in 1971. One index of public sentiment at the time was that the measure did not receive a single dissenting vote in the House of Commons.

Another recommendation that proved significant was "that a Department of Consumer Affairs headed by a Minister be established." But the committee frankly admitted its inability to smoke out any villains responsible for soaring food prices: "Your Committee's review of the evidence has not yet revealed any group or sector of the economy which could be singled out and blamed for the recent increase in food prices."[17]

There was some flattering media coverage of the committee's interim report, perhaps in part because the members of the press gallery did not have to spend endless hours wading through volumes of turgid prose to find their stories. Charles Lynch, for example, was generous in his praise:

> The report of the parliamentary prices committee is the best thing to come off the Hill in many a session and should raise the ratings of our much-maligned MPs and Senators.
>
> A more workmanlike document it would be hard to imagine, and it is all the more impressive following as it does the service the committee rendered to the public in the course of its vigorously conducted hearings.
>
> What the committee has done is to move into the vital consumer field of food, demonstrating in the process that in this area, unlike some others, governments have been too little involved.
>
> It has struck a blow for full disclosure at all levels of food marketing from the supermarket shelves to the corporate boardrooms.
>
> It has responded to the alarm bells of rising prices and come up with some preliminary answers.[18]

The committee continued with its busy schedule after Parliament reconvened and met seventeen times between 17 January and 16 February 1967. Immediately following this series of hearings, the committee split into two parts, one travelling east and the other west. Between 20 February and 1 March, these subcommittees held hearings in twelve cities and heard 197 witnesses representing ninety organizations.

At last, on 25 April 1967, the committee completed its progress report, which, in fact, turned out to be its final report. Again it was marked by brevity. It reiterated its earlier recommendation that a department of consumer affairs be established to deal with federal responsibilities for consumer standards, consumer protection and consumer information. Again special attention was devoted to the reform of packaging, grade standards and so on. The observations of the committee on rising prices continue to have some relevance and reflect the philosophic bent of its Senate cochairman:

Any general and persistent increase in the price level has a profound effect on both the economic and social fabric of a country. When the rate of increase exceeds some critical level it produces unrest and inequities and may create economic problems which have a high social cost. Parts of the population may be able to adapt to rising prices but in general these will be those who have economic or market power and whose earnings increase sufficiently fast to maintain their real income. That part of the population which is disadvantaged and economically weak will usually suffer. The handicapped, the aged, the pensioners, the underemployed and the unskilled workers bear an undue share of the burden of rising prices.[19]

Coincident with the joint committee's hearings, the federal government's responsibility in consumer affairs was also being investigated by the Economic Council. This examination stemmed from a formal request by the government in July 1966 that the council study whether the newly created Department of the Registrar General should be assigned responsibility for consumer problems. In the summer of 1967, the Economic Council issued an interim report concluding, among other things, that the primary responsibility for consumer affairs should be centred in one department. The recommendations of the joint committee were thus bolstered by the Economic Council. Accordingly, legislation was introduced in October, and the Department of Consumer and Corporate Affairs came into being that December. John Turner was its first minister. Ron Basford succeeded him in 1968.

Croll took an almost paternal pride in nearly all the committees with which he was associated in the Senate, and his fellow senators were gracious in recognizing his contribution. John Connolly, in particular, regarded Croll as an important influence on the direction of the Senate:

> Thanks to the initiative shown by Senator Croll and the members of this chamber who have served on committees which he has chaired, these last 15 years or so, the Senate has displayed a new thrust—a humanitarian thrust—a new expertise in the field of social policy, an expertise designed to benefit the poor and the aged, those people who cannot help themselves. We must all recognize that this enormous body of work has resulted in a very significant functional reform in this chamber.[20]

Plaudits for the work of the Senate committees also came from the press. In an editorial in 1978, the *Ottawa Journal* noted that "the productivity of these committees which put to public service the expertise and relative political independence of senators is the best rebuttal to grandiose schemes of Senate reform."[21]

ELEVEN

Poverty Is No Disgrace

In 1964, U.S. president Lyndon B. Johnson identified the elimination of poverty as an essential goal of the Great Society. His antipoverty campaign naturally had repercussions in Canada. The Speech from the Throne on 5 April 1965, outlining the Pearson government's pre-election legislative program, contained a Canadian commitment to banish poverty: "My Government is therefore developing a program for the full utilization of our human resources and the elimination of poverty among our people."[1]

A special planning secretariat was to be created in the Privy Council Office to deal with poverty, and a series of ambitious initiatives were announced, including improved measures for regional development, the re-employment and retraining of workers, the redevelopment of rural areas, assistance to needy people, the renewal of blighted and congested urban areas and the establishment of new opportunities for young Canadians. Heady promises indeed! Unfortunately, all this seemed to get lost in the wake of the election that followed in November, when Pearson again failed to achieve a majority government. Perhaps all the other political problems pressing in on him, and the general expectation that he would step down as prime minister and Liberal party leader before another election, caused Pearson to lose such will as he had ever possessed to complete the structure of the Canadian welfare state.

New interest in the poor and their problems would have to wait until after Pierre Elliot Trudeau, Pearson's successor as Liberal leader, had triumphed at the polls in the general election of June 1968. In the event, it was stimulated by the analysis in the *Fifth Annual Review* of the Economic Council issued that September.[2] Somewhat more restrained in its approach than President Johnson, the Economic Council limited its proposals to an attack rather than a war on poverty. And among its many useful suggestions was one that

> the Senate of Canada might consider the advisability of creating a committee to enquire into the problem of poverty in Canada. . . . The enquiry we propose would deal with all aspects of poverty, urban and rural. Many excellent witnesses, both Canadian and foreign, would be available to appear before the committee, whose work could also be aided by a small but competent research staff. The work of such a committee could do much to define and elucidate the problem of poverty in Canada, and to build public support for a more effective structure of remedial measures.[3]

On 13 September 1968, Arthur Roebuck gave notice in the Senate that Croll, whom he described as "the enterprising and forward-looking senator who is my desk mate," would present a motion calling for the appointment of a special committee on poverty.[4] Accordingly, on 8 October, Croll moved, in part,

> that a special committee of the Senate be appointed to investigate and report on all aspects of poverty in Canada, whether urban, rural, regional or otherwise, to define and elucidate the

problem of poverty in Canada, and to recommend appropriate action to ensure the establishment of a more effective structure of remedial measures;... [5]

In his explanatory remarks, Croll began with the stark statement that "the existing welfare structure is bankrupt in social purpose." He went on to stress this point:

> Public welfare is a halfway house; it has become a system of handouts, a second-rate set of social services that damages and demeans its recipients, and the program has become bankrupt. But I do not accept the specious charges that welfare lists are packed with bums, deadbeats, con men and loafers. My question is whether the welfare programs serve the poor, and effectively assist those who can be redeemed from poverty. Up to the present time it does in some way seem to have served the poor, but not very many welfare recipients have been rescued from it. The need is for the incentives which are lacking, the right to earn without penalty. These are things that must be given instant consideration.

He then sounded another note: "As a replacement for welfare there has been increasing attention to an annual guaranteed income, and although this goes deeply against religious ethics, the concept is gaining support."[6]

Later, in the discussion of his motion, Croll was able to quote from an editorial in the *Globe and Mail* of 11 November 1968:

> Almost certainly Ottawa will eventually decide that some kind of negative income tax is necessary, to put an income floor under all Canadians. This would not only alter the income tax structure, but put into a single bag a multitude of welfare programs which Ottawa now shares with the provinces

and even, in some cases, which the provinces share with the municipalities.

Someone must have been reading Croll's mind. Croll also had some support from his old associate, Paul Martin, now leader of the government in the Senate, who recalled in his autobiography:

> Early in October 1968, David Croll proposed a special Senate committee on poverty. A long-time acquaintance from his days as Mayor of Windsor in the 1930s, Croll was responding to his passionate desire for a more just society and to a proposal of the Economic Council of Canada. This was a good example of the type of work that the Senate could usefully undertake and I was right behind Croll's initiative.[7]

There was desultory debate in the Senate on Croll's motion for a couple of months before it was agreed to on 26 November.[8] The committee was to consist of seventeen members, and it was obvious that Croll would be its chairman.

The public hearings of the committee began on 22 April 1969 (appropriately with the Economic Council as its first witness) and were completed on 10 November 1970. In the interval, the committee held ninety-three public hearings. Initially, testimony came from a heavy concentration of government departments and agencies, but before it was through the committee also heard from many professional welfare organizations and other interest groups concerned with the poor. The churches, the provinces, the co-operative movement, the labour unions, the Canadian Chamber of Commerce, the Consumers' Association of Canada and the Canadian Federation of Agriculture presented briefs.

Croll was convinced that the committee should travel around the country to talk to people in their own communities. He considered it essential to meet people outside Ottawa face to face. As a result, the committee travelled from St. John's to Vancouver. Its reception, however, was not always cordial. Senator Muriel Fergusson was quoted as saying, "I was appalled when we started our tour and people yelled at us."[9] Croll, however, would have welcomed more militancy, even picketing, from the poor to call attention to the committee's work. Because of Croll's determination, the senators visited many of Canada's poor areas and looked directly in the face of poverty. Nevertheless, and without minimizing the value of this personal contact, it must be admitted that the major issues faced by the committee were conceptual and statistical and the principal contributions in these areas came from the briefs of the technically expert witnesses and the professional staff attached to the committee.

Before the committee could finish its report, however, it was pre-empted by the publication of *The Real Poverty Report*,[10] the work of four disgruntled former special committee staff members. They explained their motivation in an article in the magazine *Last Post*:

> We resigned because the chairman of the Senate Committee on Poverty [Croll] did not want to accept a candid appraisal of our society. Rather. . . it became obvious that what he really wanted was a rather maudlin discussion of what it was like to be poor, an indignant denunciation of the inadequacies of the current welfare system, followed by a call for a guaranteed annual income. He certainly did not want to tell people why they were poor.

They continued:

> The mandate given the Special Senate Committee was "to investigate and report on all aspects of poverty in Canada."

Such an investigation demands that the focus be widened to include our whole society, and to show that the economic system by which we live not only tolerates poverty, but in many ways creates, sustains, and even aggravates the problem.[11]

On the floor of the Senate Croll described the conduct of these dissidents as "outrageous" and "shocking." He said:

I am sympathetic towards the impatience of young people for action, but it is hard for me to condone behaviour that involves breaking contracts and ignoring oaths of secrecy. I do not believe that ethics have gone out of style, and both my colleagues and myself believe that unethical conduct does very little to aid the cause of the poor in this country.[12]

The authors in question may not have realized that a committee of Parliament has considerable powers of retaliation. Or perhaps they guessed correctly that the Senate would not pursue the matter of their breaches of contract and privilege. In any event, Croll and his Senate colleagues chose to endure the political embarrassment rather than prolong the adverse publicity engendered by their book.

Despite these unexpected problems in its writing, the report of the special senate committee, entitled simply *Poverty in Canada*, was tabled by Croll on 10 November 1971, and it was not long before the first printing was sold out. Although the committee ranged widely in its report, three of its recommendations stand out. The first was a guaranteed annual income, bringing under one umbrella the various schemes for income maintenance such as Old Age Security pensions and the Guaranteed Income Supplement, Family and Youth Allowances, Occupational Training Allowances and other special allowances. Social insurance schemes with an actuarial basis such as Unemployment Insurance, Workmen's Compensation and the Canada/Quebec Pension Plan would continue their independent existence. The committee's second major proposal was to establish a single, national official poverty line to provide a benchmark for measuring the extent and the trend of poverty in the country. Without going into the technical details of its computation, the poverty line used by the Senate committee is roughly 50 per cent of the average disposable personal annual income in Canada, adjusted for family size. It therefore has the great advantage of automatically reflecting changes in such basic economic variables as total output and price movements, as well as changing patterns of family size. Finally, the committee recommended that 70 per cent of the poverty line be established immediately as the guaranteed annual income (GAI) for all Canadians but that this level be increased as rapidly as possible to 100 per cent. On the subject of the administrative machinery required to implement its proposals, the committee was impressed with the advantages of adapting the income tax system for broader purposes than revenue collection. Consequently, it adopted the proposals of the American economist Milton Friedman and suggested that the most effective technique would be a negative income tax.

Initially, it seemed that these recommendations might significantly affect government policy. Indeed, the Speech from the Throne on 17 February 1972 contained the following:

> It is the view of the Government that the most important single factor in the attainment of individual dignity and active social involvement is the assurance of a secure income. Considerable progress towards the goal of a total income security programme for all Canadians is achieved in the new Family Income Security Plan bill which will be presented for your consideration. The emphasis in this plan is on protection and is consistent with the Government's belief in the strong sense of self-reliance of Canadians.[13]

This encouraging note to the contrary, the guaranteed annual income was not forthcoming.

Croll sounded slightly discouraged in remarks to the Senate in the spring of 1972:

> What troubles me is that the message we attempted to get across in our report has not gotten across. As soon as a guaranteed income is mentioned, you hear "Oh, free ride; pie in the sky; everybody gets something for nothing, and away we go." If you take a few minutes to read the report you would know that the guaranteed annual income is subject to work incentives, earning incentives, and tax incentives; it is not just a handout.[14]

In 1974, however, when Croll returned to the issue of poverty and the guaranteed annual income in his Address in Reply to the Speech from the Throne, he was able to claim that the concept of the GAI had been generally accepted. Public opinion polls now indicated that 60 per cent of the people agreed with the idea, and he noted that the United Church of Canada had endorsed the concept.

It would be difficult to improve on Croll's assessment, given in the Senate in 1984, of the subsequent history of the *Poverty in Canada* report:

> Honourable senators, today [29 May 1984] you found in your office the 1984 edition of the Report of the Special Senate Committee on Poverty in Canada. It has just come off the press and it is in both official languages. The report was first printed in 1971 and reprinted in 1972, 1974, 1976, 1980 and 1984 in both official languages, for a total of 28,500 copies. It is indeed a landmark report. It did not solve the problem of poverty, but it has made thousands of people in Canada, who

were not poverty stricken, aware of the problem and it has been an inspiration to many. This year's reprint was for 1,000 copies, bringing the total, as I said, to 28,500 copies printed. The 1,000 copies of the report were given away to government ministries across the country, government departments, libraries, universities and provincial departments that requested copies. Over the years, the report has sold at prices beginning in 1971 at $1, increasing to $3, $5, and $7. The present price is $7.95 and outside this country it costs $9.95. It is the single most popular parliamentary report printed since 1867. . . .

More copies of this report have been printed and sold than any other single report in the history of this country. It has made a vital contribution over the years to the relief of poverty, a contribution which has been considerable and noteworthy. It is used as a text book and research document in every university in Canada and has made a great impression on the Canadian people.

The report is the exclusive product of this chamber. It is a combined effort and stands to the credit of the totality of this place and indicates the type of work we can do in a proper environment. Particular thanks are due to the late Senator John Connolly, and Senator Perrault and Senator Flynn who encouraged and supported the study. The original number of members on the committee was 20. Eight members are in the house at the present time, four are retired and eight have passed on. It is appropriate that I inscribe the names of the committee members still in this chamber. They are: Senators Rhéal Bélisle, Eric Cook, Douglas D. Everett, Earl A. Hastings, Elsie Inman, Fred A. McGrand, Herbert O. Sparrow and myself.

This report has stood the test of time by describing as the poverty line an amount that is approximately 50 per cent of the average Canadian family income, adjusted to family size and making provision for inflation and gross national product. It has been widely approved and copied. Moreover, a Member of Parliament, who is a candidate for the Liberal leadership, the Honourable Donald Johnston, has made it part of his interesting platform to combine social assistance programs into one guaranteed income plan. We did not invent the guaranteed income in our report, but 15 years ago we got it off the ground as a social and political movement. We made the idea of it respected, practical and acceptable.

I should point out that in addition to the reports, we have printed more than 10,000 booklets highlighting the major parts of the various reports to send to people who could not afford the expense of the full reports. We ran out of those very quickly.

All in all, honourable senators, it was good day's work for the Senate. The report which the honourable senators have is worthy of placement in home libraries.

After 15 years, one wonders whether the time has come for the updating of the report through new eyes.[15]

The annual Senate Poverty Line update, however, remains Croll's precious jewel, and he has been assiduous in nurturing and publicizing the committee's benchmark. On 23 January 1990, for example, he tabled in the Senate the eighteenth revision of the data, including a forecast for 1989. The actual figures for 1988 showed that the dividing line for a family of three had increased to $22,000 from $6,145 in 1974—a startling increase. For 1988, the tables showed that 20.9 per cent of the population was living below the Senate Poverty Line. In December 1985, in a column in the *Globe and Mail*, June Callwood noted that the Senate's concern with poverty continued, mainly as a result of Croll's efforts. She referred to him as a "national treasure."[16]

TWELVE

Retirement without Tears

NOT UNRELATED TO THE PROBLEMS OF AGING AND POV-
erty was the question of retirement and its associated problems, which stirred widespread interest in North America in
the late 1970s. There were several reasons for this interest.
Probably the most significant was the increase in prices trig-
gered by the oil crisis in 1973–74. The damage to those on
fixed incomes, particularly the elderly poor, caused general
concern. Another reason was the series of congressional hearings in the United States, which greatly emphasized the in-
fringement of human rights resulting from age discrimination
and generated a spate of publicity. In 1978, amendments to
the U.S. Age Discrimination in Employment Act of 1967
were passed that extended mandatory retirement in the private sector from sixty-five to seventy and abolished compulsory retirement for U.S. federal employees.

Human rights were also in the forefront in Canada, and
many of the provinces were concerned with age discrimination in employment, although protective legislation usually
stopped at sixty-five. A rash of public inquiries, as well as numerous private studies, including articles and monographs,
stimulated public interest in retirement and allied issues.

On 15 November 1977, Croll introduced a motion in the Senate calling for the creation of a committee to explore all aspects of public and private policies concerning retirement age. After a debate lasting several weeks, the Senate approved Croll's motion, which contained the following order of reference, in part:

> That a special committee of the Senate be appointed to examine and report on
> (a) the existing retirement age policies affecting workers in both the public and the private sectors;
> (b) the social and economic implications of mandatory retirement based on age alone;
> (c) the feasibility of enabling workers, especially elderly citizens, to continue to make a worthwhile contribution to our society through flexible voluntary retirement plans to the extent of their ability and motivation;
> (d) the protection of those over sixty-five against age discrimination in all employment areas; and
> (e) the need for the maximum co-operation of all levels of government, labour unions and the public in respect of existing and future retirement age policies and retirement plans;... [1]

The committee, known as the Special Senate Committee on Retirement Age Policies, was composed of twenty-two senators.

A small research and planning staff was appointed early in 1978 to draw up a list of witnesses and prepare invitations. Because of the lead time required, hearings were not scheduled until after the summer recess. Parliament reconvened on 11 October 1978, and shortly thereafter the committee hearings began.

Much of the testimony before the committee on the subjects of aging and retirement corroborated information assembled by earlier committees. Some of the experts in gerontology claimed that a person who was sixty-five in 1978 was physically equivalent to someone forty-five or fifty years old just a few generations earlier. As the Special Senate Committee on Aging had noted some years before, dramatic advances in medicine, a better diet and the fact that many workers no longer spent their lives at punishing physical labour made the difference.

The committee was to conclude that mandatory retirement at sixty-five was unjust and unwarranted as a general rule and that it led to enormous losses in the productive capacity of the economy. The committee believed that specific steps could be taken to encourage a more flexible approach to retirement age. The federal and the provincial governments could modify the retirement policies applicable to their own employees. Human rights legislation, both federal and provincial, could be modified where necessary to eliminate discrimination based on age. While the committee's view was that there is nothing sacred about the custom of dismissing people from their work on their sixty-fifth birthday, it agreed that the process of change should be gradual to minimize disruption in such fields as pensions, disability insurance and group life insurance.

At a very early stage, Croll and the other committee members saw that one of the essentials for successful retirement, when this was deemed desirable by the individual concerned, was a comfortable income. With good health and a decent income, retired people had a reasonable chance of spending their retirement years in dignity. This committee, like its predecessors on aging and poverty, had to face the disturbing fact that poverty was prevalent among the elderly. At the time of the hearings, there were about 1.2 million Canadians over sixty-five receiving the Guaranteed Income Supplement to the Old Age Security pension, something only paid to those in need. This amounted to about half the old age pensioners. On the basis of such statistics, the emphasis of the committee shifted to the consideration of retirement income. It was not sensible to deal with the issue of mandatory retirement without looking at the problem of income at the same time, in particular at the adequacy of private pensions, as well as of the Canada/Quebec Pension Plan (c/QPP).

The principal conclusions of the committee on private pensions were:

> that the private pension plan system in Canada has serious shortcomings with respect to coverage, benefits, vesting, portability and indexing as well as in its treatment of particular groups in the population such as women and part-time workers; [and] that the regulations governing vesting in private pension plans are, in general, too restrictive;... [2]

The committee was equally unequivocal in its recommendation that the c/QPP be expanded and liberalized. It proposed that the aggregate contributions should be increased to 8 per cent and concluded that the c/QPP should become the main instrument for overhauling the pension system in Canada. The plan had the highly desirable characteristics of immediate vesting, portability, tax deductibility, indexing and universality.

One of the most difficult issues faced by the committee was that of women and pensions. In 1977, 60 per cent of unattached women over sixty-five had incomes below the poverty line. It is projected that by the end of the century, there will be over two million women in Canada over the age of sixty-five, almost double the number in 1980.

The committee was critical of the treatment of women by

private pension plans. Health and Welfare Canada estimates of the average annual income of all women sixty-six and over from private pensions, including superannuation income and annuities, amounted to a pitiful $370. This low figure is a result, in part, of the small number of women in the labour force participating in private pension plans. There was also some outright discrimination. Some schemes did not admit women or provided for their entry at an older age and retirement at a younger age than men. The mandatory retirement age for women was often fixed at sixty, whereas men were kept on until sixty-five. The adequacy of survivors' benefits was also looked at with disapproval by the committee. Federal public service and other pension plans left the widow to enjoy 50 per cent of her late husband's pension or provided no survivors' benefits or allowed the husband to opt out of providing them.

The committee had as well to consider the tangled question of how to treat housewives under the c/QPP. They made an obvious contribution to the economy, but they didn't work for pay and could not be brought into the pension plan under established concepts. Voluntary contributions were inequitable, since they would discriminate against lower-income groups. The committee believed the best solution was to provide for sharing pensions between husbands and wives on a nondiscriminatory basis.

The last paragraph of the committee's report read:

The number of elderly people will increase and more and more people of all ages will have to deal with the social issues that result. A helpful and compassionate approach is needed but this will only come with public appreciation of the twin problems of retirement and income. Your Committee believes that the subject of this report is a major social issue just as important as Old Age Security and Medicare. It is earnestly hoped that this report will contribute to the understanding of the

Canadian people and, in particular, their essential role in building a social structure that will be the envy of the western world.[3]

The target date for the tabling of the final report *Retirement without Tears* was 19 December 1979, almost exactly two years after the approval of Croll's original resolution. However, Prime Minister Clark's government was defeated on 13 December, so the plans had to be revised. The report was released on schedule but was not formally tabled in the Senate until 15 April 1980.

It was not the tabling of *Retirement without Tears* but the unrelated entrenchment of the Canadian Charter of Rights and Freedoms in the Constitution on 17 April 1982 that finally offered a solution to the problem of compulsory retirement. In particular, section 15, dealing with equality rights, provided for safeguards against discrimination on a number of grounds, including age:

> Every individual is equal before and under the law and has the right to the equal protection and equal benefit of the law without discrimination and, in particular, without discrimination based on race, national or ethnic origin, colour, religion, sex, age or mental or physical disability.

It would appear, however, that any proposal to bolster the c/QPP will continue to run into powerful opposition from two influential quarters, the pension industry and small business. Although increases in contributions may be contemplated from time to time to protect the solvency of the system, the committee's proposal to make the c/QPP pensions a major part of income maintenance for the retired is unlikely ever to be implemented.

Croll, however, was never one to give up. If he couldn't

persuade the government to adopt a responsible social policy on the problems of aging in Canada, perhaps he could so awaken the consciousness of all Canadians to their obligations in this regard that the government would be forced to act. In the spring of 1987, he reiterated his call for increased recognition of the elderly by introducing a resolution in the Senate that called for the establishment of a senior citizens' week during the last complete week in August. This would be a time to pay tribute to the elderly. He was eloquent in describing the debt society owed to its senior citizens:

> One of the most important features of western society is the enormous heritage of social capital left to us by our ancestors, to which we have added from time to time. Our parents were motivated by affection as well as a sense of duty to provide for the material welfare of their children.
>
> In those days, immigrants often arrived in Canada with little more than the clothes on their backs, but they gave their children a good education, and, within a generation, many of them were able to pass on to their children prosperous farms or businesses.
>
> The inheritance of private wealth is important, but it does not compare to the huge accumulation of social capital passed down from earlier times. There is much talk these days about what we owe to our children and our grandchildren. I am more concerned at the moment about how much we owe to the elderly who have given us so much within living memory. Young people take for granted the priceless gift of arable land, roads, utilities, hospitals, schools, museums and stately public buildings that contribute so much to the general welfare. Some of the outstanding contributors to our well-being, even politicians, are recognized and honoured. Usually when they

are dead we name schools, parks, mountains and even high-
ways after them. This doubtless pleases their living descen-
dants, but it would also be pleasant and fitting if we could
honour some of the other contributors to our society while
they are still with us.[4]

When St. Thomas University in Fredericton, New Brunswick, awarded Croll the degree of Doctor of Laws *honoris
causa* at its 1980 spring convocation, it was an occasion to eu-
logize some of Croll's achievements:

His consistent deep commitment to alleviating the pain of
poverty and enhancing the dignity of labour has governed a
lifetime of vigorous activity, from his precedent-setting work
on Windsor's relief system during the depression to his chairmanship, in the seventies, of the Senate Committee on Poverty, and from his creation of the Minimum Wage Act in Ontario to his recent chairmanship of the Senate Committee on
Retirement Age Policies. It is difficult to believe that any Canadian has been more consistently active in these areas or has
had a greater impact on our attitude toward, and our treatment of, the impoverished and the dispossessed.

And Toronto's Baycrest Centre Foundation, which sup-
ports a Jewish home for the aged and a hospital, established
the *Chai* (Life) Award to be presented to individuals who
have made outstanding contributions in their fields of endeavour after the age of sixty-five. So far, show business personality George Burns and Croll are its only recipients. The Foundation had earlier recognized Croll's efforts to better the lives
of older people by appointing him a lifetime honorary governor.

THIRTEEN

Family Matters and Other Adventures

THE CHERNIAK/CROLL CONNECTION EXPANDED AND PROS-
pered in Windsor and Detroit as well as in other cities.

The Croll family in Windsor that emigrated in 1905 and
1906 was bound by strong ties of affection. Minka Croll was
the focus of family life when the children were growing up and
afterwards. She was widely known in the family connection as
Auntie Minka. She was a true matriarchal figure.

David's brother Leo was next to him in age. After Leo graduated from the Windsor Collegiate Institute, he entered the
University of Michigan Medical School in 1921 and graduated in 1925 with the degree of M.D. He was an intern at the
Baltimore General Hospital and took his residency at the
Brooklyn Eye and Ear Hospital, specializing in ophthalmology. He served in the United States Army in the period
1942–46 as chief of ophthalmology at Fort Benjamin Harri-
son and then returned to private practice in Detroit. He was
still practising in the mid 1980s; he died on 22 January 1989.

The next brother, Samuel, graduated in dentistry after attending both the University of Michigan and the University
of Toronto and practised for many years near Detroit until his
death on 3 January 1981.

Maurice, the first of the brothers born in Canada, also entered the University of Michigan as a dental student. He graduated in 1927 with a D.D.S. He then changed his mind and decided to enroll in the Wayne State University Medical School to study ophthalmology and in due course received an M.D. He also took his residency at the Brooklyn Eye and Ear Hospital in 1940–42. During World War II he was a flight surgeon with the Air Transport Command of the United States Air Force for two years. He became a member of the faculty of the Kresge Eye Institute at Wayne State University and chief of the Ophthalmology and Otolaryngology Department at Grace Hospital, Detroit. After the war, he also joined his brother Leo in private practice in Detroit. Before his retirement, he spent part of each summer treating South American Indians, usually in Brazil. He has been described as a novelist, comedian, neighbourhood philosopher, eye doctor and poet in Hebrew, Yiddish and English.

The youngest brother, Cecil, followed in David's legal footsteps. He practised law in Windsor, first in David's firm, then as a partner in Croll and Croll and later on his own after David left Windsor.

The only girl in the family was Evelyn. She was trained as a dental hygienist. She married an accountant, David P. Zack, and lived in Detroit, where she and her husband were prominent in community affairs. In 1977 the couple was honoured at the annual awards dinner of the Jewish National Fund. On this occasion the David P. and Evelyn Zack Forest was established in their honour in the American Bicentennial National Park in Israel. Evelyn died on 16 February 1985 in her seventy-fourth year.

Sarah Croll's family members had distinguished careers in Detroit and Michigan. Of her five brothers, Theodore, Saul and Bayre became lawyers and established the firm of Levin, Levin and Dill. Theodore later became a federal judge in

Michigan. Sam became a doctor and Hoke a merchant. Sarah also had two younger sisters. One of Sarah Croll's nephews, Carl Levin, was elected a Democratic senator from Michigan in 1978 and again in 1984. Another was Michigan Supreme Court Justice Charles Levin. Two of the other nephews were elected members of the House of Representatives.

The three girls born to David and Sarah Croll, Eunice, Constance and Sandra, all carried on the family tradition and went on to university and later careers in addition to raising families.

Eunice graduated from the University of Toronto in social work. On 22 September 1948, she married David Mouckley, the son of Mr. and Mrs. Nathan Mouckley, in Holy Blossom Temple in Toronto, and had three children.

Constance went to Vassar and on 18 June 1946 married Ira Young, who was in the real estate business in Edmonton, but they were later divorced. There were three children by this marriage.

Sandra started college at the University of Michigan but transferred after a couple of years to the University of Toronto. She graduated with an Honours B.A. in history. On 10 February 1955, she was married to Frederick Ralph Papsin, the son of Mr. and Mrs. George Papsin. A medical student at the time, he became a prominent gynecologist in Toronto. The couple had four children.

By 1990 Croll had ten grandchildren and a rapidly growing crop of great-grandchildren.

Both Hillel and Minka Croll survived long enough to see all three of David's children married and to enjoy at least some of their great-grandchildren. In Hillel Croll's old age, he badly wanted to visit Israel. His wife, however, did not share his enthusiasm for such a pilgrimage. It was clear to the family that he wished to stay in Israel, and he would not promise to come back after a visit. As a result, his family, particularly David, persuaded him to abandon the project.

Hillel Croll retired from all business activities about 1940 and was able to visit the *shul* three times a day. He attended services in the morning, afternoon and evening and was able to enjoy the companionship of ten or twelve others of like mind. In addition, there were almost always a few people in the synagogue saying prayers in remembrance of relatives or friends. He devoted himself to looking after the welfare work of the congregation and spent his time visiting the sick and looking after the poor. When he died on 23 November 1955, he had been a highly respected worker for the religious and social welfare of the Jews in Windsor for fifty years. He was probably about eighty at the time of his death. In one of the newspapers the obituary said:

> Mr. and Mrs. Croll worked with and for their city as well as their family and scarcely a welfare group exists among the Jewish people in which both did not participate, as well as giving their constant support to other community welfare efforts.[1]

At the funeral service, Rabbi Samuel Stollman of Shaar Hashomayim Synagogue said that Hillel Croll was noted for his piety, his respect for his fellow men and his charity. He said that "his life will always remain a shining light in the chronicles of Jewish life in this community."[2]

Minka Croll was spared for many years to savour the achievements of her children and their progeny but finally succumbed on 30 July 1970 at the age of about ninety.[3] At the time of her death, she had thirteen grandchildren and fourteen great-grandchildren.

Croll was saddened by the death of his mother to whom he owed so much for her lifelong support and encouragement.

But his greater sorrow was to come with the death of Sally, his wife for more than sixty years. She had been in failing health for some time, although she remained alert and interested until the end. She died on 26 May 1987, a month or so before her eighty-fourth birthday. She was a handsome and intelligent woman who had made significant contributions to worthy causes all her adult life and was greatly loved by her children and their children. This sad event meant a drastic change in Croll's life, which had focussed on his wife's health during her final illness. Despite the support of his family and friends, he was upset by the trauma of loss, complicated by some of the inevitable physical problems of beginning old age.

After Croll's second daughter, Connie, married Ira Young in 1946, the couple lived in Edmonton, where Young was a business associate of Samuel Belzberg. Because they were also neighbours, an intimate social relationship developed between the two families. When Croll went to Edmonton to visit his daughter, son-in-law and grandchildren in the 1950s, he naturally came to know Sam Belzberg and his brothers, Bill and Hyman. At the time, Sam and Bill were principally involved in real estate, with some interests in gas and oil and pet food. Hyman ran the family furniture store, founded by their father. The brothers looked up to Croll, not only because he was a distinguished senator but also because they needed the services of a lawyer who knew his way around Ottawa. At this stage in their careers, the Belzberg brothers operated in a restricted sphere and were seeking more efficient methods of financing their operations.

Acting on their behalf, Croll went to see Kenneth R. McGregor, the federal superintendent of insurance, who, among his other duties, was responsible for the supervision of federally incorporated trust companies. McGregor's advice was that the Belzbergs incorporate a trust company under the laws of Alberta. As a result, the City Savings and Trust Company was incorporated by an act of the Alberta legislature on 5 April 1962. Croll was designated chairman of the board. Sam Belzberg was president, and Bill Belzberg vice-president. Among the directors was Croll's friend and fellow senator, Allister Grosart (a Conservative). The first meeting of the board took place around the kitchen table in the Belzberg home in Edmonton.

Later the name of the company was changed to First City Trust, and City Savings and Trust became a subsidiary. The new trust company pioneered bridge or interim financing in Western Canada, which was a great help to builders when their money was tied up in current construction. It was also one of the first trust companies to establish a subsidiary solely devoted to leasing. After Sam Belzberg moved to Vancouver in 1968, a holding company, First City Financial Corporation, was incorporated in British Columbia. Croll again was chairman of the board. In 1972, the common shares of both First City Financial Corporation and First City Trust were listed on the Toronto Stock Exchange. The affairs of First City Financial Corporation have prospered, and subsidiaries have been established in the United States. In early 1987, a new financial holding company, First City Trustco Inc., acquired the common shares of First City Trust. When he was seventy-five, Croll stepped down as chairman of the board of First City Trust but continued as chairman of First City Financial Corporation until 1983. In both corporations, he remains honorary chairman.[4]

When he was sixty-five, Croll made an elaborate junket to the Soviet Union and Czechoslovakia and was able to combine it with a pilgrimage to his place of birth. This experience had a profound impact on him. The occasion was the visit of a parliamentary delegation in response to an official invitation from the Supreme Soviet of the U.S.S.R. and the chairman of the National Assembly of the Czechoslovak Socialist Republic. The visit was to include a stay in the Soviet Union from 19 July to 30 July 1965 and in Czechoslovakia from 30 July to 7 August. There were fourteen parliamentarians from Canada, including two senators. Alan MacNaughton, the speaker of the House of Commons, was one cochairman of the delegation and Croll the other. Croll was representing the Speaker of the Senate, Maurice Bourget, who was not able to make the trip.

Soviet officialdom showed the Canadians the warmest hospitality. The group had a brief visit with Alexei Kosygin, chairman of the Council of Ministers, and Croll was able to express the opinion to him that a bridge of understanding would be built between Moscow and Ottawa that would ultimately result in a bridge to world peace.[5] Anastas Mikoyan, the chairman of the Presidium of the Supreme Soviet of the U.S.S.R., had longer to spend with the guests. They also saw Yanis V. Pieve, chairman of the Council of Nationalities of the Supreme Soviet of the U.S.S.R. The itinerary of the delegation was breathtaking, since they also visited Kiev, Leningrad, Moscow, Tbilisi and Sochi, a resort on the Black Sea. There were the usual obligatory visits to factories and monuments as well as official receptions. Croll, through the interpreter, told his hosts repeatedly that many Canadians of Slavic origin felt emotional ties to their homeland and were not necessarily antagonistic to the Soviet Union.[6]

But for Croll himself, the high point of the visit was his trip to Teterina, the *shtetl* near Mogilev where he was born. The Russians recognized that Croll was a very special person, "a Byelorussian boy who had made good in the New World."[7] Presumably at the instigation of the Canadian Embassy, the Ministry of Foreign Affairs provided him with a car, a driver and an interpreter and sent him off from Moscow in search of his origins. The distance from Moscow to Mogilev is about

1100 kilometres, but there was a good, broad highway and very little traffic.

It was reported that the villagers were more fascinated by the Volga automobile that Croll travelled in than by the white-haired gentleman from Canada. Croll observed that "the town was the same as when I left it—chickens, goats and children playing in the main street. Of course, the roads aren't paved: never were and probably never will be."[8] The main street was little more than a wagon track. There was even a story about Croll's return in the Russian press. The Novosti press agency reported that he climbed a hill at the edge of the village but was unable to find his parents' house. The place had been levelled during World War II and most of the inhabitants murdered by the Nazis. Novosti quoted Croll as saying, "The Fascists destroyed everything here, but they were unable to vanquish the people." Croll did find a school-teacher with an interest in genealogy who had some old records of the family, but the relations had been killed during the war or scattered.

FOURTEEN

Winding Down

DONALD CREIGHTON REFERRED TO SENATE REFORM AS "one of the stalest and most fraudulent exercises in Canadian politics."[1] The Senate has been a traditional whipping boy, and denouncing it has at various times past appeared to be a qualification for membership in the CCF or in its more recent incarnation, the New Democratic Party. As Canada enters the 1990s, Senate reform has become a cause célèbre.

Throughout his years in the Senate, Croll himself has made numerous proposals concerning its reform. His defence of and observations about the chamber beginning in the fall of 1968 seem, however, of particular value in the context of this latest Senate reform controversy:

There are professional belittlers of the Senate who continue to play, repetitiously, a cracked record about this body. They do not know what they are talking about. The Senate which they condemned does not live here any more. It has not been here for about ten years. The reformation began quietly in its own way. It is being done from within. In my view there is nothing wrong with the Senate that more work and responsibility would not cure. To date we have never been tested; our potential has never been totally used. It is time we stopped apologizing for the Senate, particularly for the Senate which no longer exists.[2]

He gave a long critical analysis of the work of the Senate early in 1969 and returned to one of his favourite topics, the advantages of committee operations: "The greatest strength that we have in the Senate and have had for a long time is our committees. Our committees gave us character, a solidarity and we were blessed with chairmen of unusual ability. . . ."[3] He applauded the work of Senators Hugessen, Roebuck and Thorvaldson as chairmen of Senate committees and described the impact of some of the Senate committees' recommendations on legislation. He dated the investigatory functions of the committees to around 1957, when the Special Senate Committee on Land Use began its work, although a closer examination might show that valuable investigations were carried out at a much earlier date.

Croll claimed that the Senate could conduct many of the investigations needed by the government. Royal commissions could be dispensed with, except perhaps in special cases such as the circumstances that prompted the appointment of the Royal Commission on Bilingualism and Biculturalism. The advantages of using Senate committees would be economy, the continuing nature of the Senate, which is not affected by parliamentary mortality, and the fact that the Senate is in a position to follow up the recommendations of its committees with legislative initiatives, if necessary.

Croll then outlined the various current proposals, as he had gleaned them from "gossip and newspaper reports":

I think what is being considered are these matters: First, should there be a time limit? Should a time limit be fixed for service in the Senate—say, about 20 years? Then, what should the term of new appointments be, three years, six years or 10 years? Should an appointee be eligible for reappointment? Should there be provincial appointments, and how many? Should provincial appointments be made by the premier of the province or from a panel presented by the premier of the province to the Prime Minister who makes the appointment? What new special powers should the Senate be given to deal with the official languages bills, human rights, and treaty obligations? Should the Senate be given power to approve new appointments such as Supreme Court judges, ambassadors, heads of agencies, cultural and otherwise—a sort of advice and consent as modified under the American system. Should the veto be removed and a delaying power only given to the Senate, and how should that be limited, and how to preserve a built-in majority for the government of the day?[4]

He returned to the theme of Senate reform in the spring of 1973, this time in a reminiscent mood. He spoke of his time in the House of Commons, when he did not regard the Senate with favour:

Frankly, the Senate was not my cup of tea; in modern language, it was not my bag. I had been used to the cut and thrust of politics. I liked the House of Commons. It suited my temperament, and I felt at home there.[5]

He then went on to make some observations about the discriminatory treatment of minorities in the appointment of senators:

If you understand my background as a member of an immigrant minority you will understand that there are pressures unseen, but very real and very worthy. There is an overriding sense of obligation to open doors which have traditionally been closed, and to provide opportunities for new Canadians to fully join the Canadian family. The most effective way is to get elected to Parliament. That is acceptance. It sets the tone because it is Parliament. I need not tell you that to us minorities there were bolted doors that had to be unbolted and unlocked. People of my tradition suffered the most for doors were slammed in their faces. After 80 years the anglophones and francophones, who had had this Senate all to themselves, finally let us come in out of the cold to join the Senate, and to show that we can take our place alongside our fellow Canadians who were the founding fathers.[6]

Croll had learned at an early age to mind his social and political manners. Consequently, in his maiden speech in the Senate in 1955, he was effusive about the honour and the privilege, and so on. By 1973, he no longer found it necessary to dissemble:

I came to the Senate in 1955. I must tell you I was bored and frustrated. It was an intolerable situation. There were great men in here, fine men. No one would dare use any but the finest words in speaking of them, and they did not neglect their responsibilities or their duties. We met, we prayed, and we adjourned. They were old and they were coasting. There was a small group, an oligarchy, which conducted the business. We were young, we were fresh, and we were anxious. We came to serve and we remained to sit, and history is repeating itself now. Many here sit who came to serve; there has not been much change in that respect. . . .

The Senate at the time was in the public eye mistrusted, misunderstood, in many circles disliked and written off; in any event at a very low ebb. The administration, as I have indicated, was in the hands of a competent, capable, but chosen few. There was no response to change. All important posts were allotted, all interesting assignments were designated, and all junkets spoken for. They were very well organized to do nothing more than rubber stamp that which the Commons sent over, although I must say they did it with great flourish and some very fine speeches.[7]

Croll then delivered a careful, detailed analysis of the recent accomplishments of the Senate, with particular emphasis on its committees and the joint committees over the last fifteen years, and outlined his own twelve-point program for Senate reform (although he freely admitted that much of it was not original). He proposed that a limited suspensive veto replace the absolute veto power of the Senate over legislation, that the geographical distribution of senators be adjusted, that no political party compose more than two thirds of the Senate at any one time, that the compulsory retirement age for senators be reduced to seventy, that the government leader in the Senate not be a member of cabinet, that age restrictions be imposed on some of the principal officers of the Senate, plus some minor recommendations on the detailed operations of the chamber. His proposals were received amicably enough by many of his colleagues. Senator Connolly again paid tribute to Croll's enterprise:

I suppose it should surprise no one in the chamber that Senator Croll should sponsor a debate on Senate reform. Since the honorable senator entered this chamber in 1955, he has been a reformer. Many of his earlier ideas were branded as unorthodox, and I might say that I have lived to see many of those ideas become respected and accepted in very respectable quarters.[8]

On the question of an elected Senate, Croll has concluded that it will take some years before this proposal becomes a practical matter. He cannot imagine any prime minister abandoning the political leverage of an appointed Senate, except in the face of overwhelming public demand. In an aside during a 1985 Senate address on the subject of justice for the elderly, he took aim at the Senate's many angry critics, and at Conservative minister of justice John Crosbie in particular, to suggest that the question of Senate reform be referred directly to the Canadian people. Scornful of past, trifling opinion surveys, he proposed that a national referendum find out from all Canadians whether they wanted to abolish the Senate or how they wanted it reformed.[9]

By the time he had reached his eighties, Croll began to curtail his busy schedule. His attendance in the Senate was faithful, but his participation in the work of its committees tapered off when his term as chairman of the Special Senate Committee on Retirement Age Policies ended. Despite various opportunities, he was reluctant to take on any new major projects. He is content to participate in those Senate activities that interest him and to continue issuing his annual revisions of the Senate Poverty Line.

The constitutional issues that surfaced in the early 1980s, however, were as meat and drink to him. During the long debate on the patriation of the constitution in 1981, Croll was able to review many of the social issues with which he had been involved. He disclaimed any wish to deal with the technical aspects of constitutional law but spoke of the pioneer work that he and Diefenbaker and Coldwell had undertaken to promote a bill of rights years before. The proposed Canadian Charter of Rights and Freedoms, which was ultimately to be entrenched in the Constitution, was intended to protect the disadvantaged, the disabled, women, aboriginal people and the foreign-born. To Croll, the entrenchment of these

rights meant "unbelievable progress," which he had not anticipated in this century. He spoke in particular for the 35 per
cent of the population who were neither English nor French
in origin when he quoted from his speech in the House of
Commons about thirty-five years earlier on the citizenship issue:

> We have not come, in the main, from some dark European
> morass where learning or culture never flowered. It was not ig-
> norance that led us to reject our homes and our friends and
> the countries of our birth—and out of all lands to which we
> might have gone, to choose Canada. We, or our fathers, were
> actuated by these same impulses which, one or two or three
> centuries earlier, had led the forebears of the hon. members,
> whether they speak English or French, to make this same ven-
> turesome, sometimes desperate, move from an old world to a
> new, to escape from drudgery without hope of security, hunger
> born of social injustice, religious faith without the freedom to
> practise it, democratic idealism ruthlessly suppressed by the
> despot. . . . [10]

He closed on an equally eloquent note:

> My pioneering days are almost over, but before my political
> career comes entirely to a close, I would like to see my dream
> come true, of a strong and just Canada, independent and
> united, proud in its diversity rather than strained in its dissen-
> sion. That would be a confirmation, not only of my dreams
> but also the dreams of all Canadians. [11]

Unhappily, Croll's euphoric mood was shattered by the
changes insisted on by the provinces at a federal/provincial
conference in the fall of 1981. Compromises had to be made,

and the new rules provided that provinces could pass legislation that would override the Charter of Rights and Freedoms. Croll was bitter about this development and claimed that the provinces had shot the charter full of holes.

> Provincial premiers unjustifiably taking on the right to speak for all citizens on all matters have emasculated the Charter to protect their own powers and advance the interest of their bureaucracies. [12]

He then went on:

> One of the prime objectives of the Charter was supposed to be national unity—equal rights and equal treatment for all Canadians from sea to sea. Now the rights will vary from province to province in a legal crazy quilt. This is a shattering blow to national unity. [13]

He thought the federal government had given away too much, and he was badly disappointed. He believed the provincial premiers had "messed things up" and that the spectre of balkanization remained. However, he ended on a warm note by congratulating Trudeau and Chrétien for their accomplishment.

In fact, Croll had long been a supporter of Trudeau. In the mid-1960s, when Trudeau emerged from relative obscurity, he seemed like a breath of fresh air to Croll. He appreciated Trudeau's incisive style in caucus and admired his Jesuitical capacity to demolish an illogical or specious argument. Croll believed that Trudeau's intellectual toughness was essential to the rejuvenation of the Liberal party.

At the Liberal leadership convention in the spring of 1968, Trudeau's supporters from the Senate numbered only three:

Croll, Eric Cook from Newfoundland and Sarto Fournier from Montreal. In a letter to the *Toronto Daily Star* on 9 March 1968, Croll described his reasons for supporting Trudeau:

> Pierre Elliott Trudeau is a new young face, a professional, who brings to the problems of today a trained mind, a clear grasp of principle, and a freedom from preconceived ideas. . . .
>
> It is said that Mr. Trudeau is inexperienced. Here is a successful lawyer, a successful teacher, a completely successful parliamentarian. More is needed to make a great prime minister than long residence in the House of Commons. We need a prime minister without blinkers; a man who is not enslaved by commitments to group or region or faction; someone who is his own man. . . .
>
> I believe that Mr. Trudeau can rally around him and lead a new updated Liberal party that includes the best and strongest of the parliamentary Liberal party while attracting the best men and women from every province and walk of life, as well as inducing the strays to return to the fold. . . .
>
> I believe that Pierre Elliott Trudeau is a winner and will be good for Canada.

Croll was also able to persuade some of his wealthy friends to contribute generously to the Trudeau cause.

Croll's admiration for Trudeau continued over the years of their association. The birth of Trudeau's first son, Justin, on 25 December 1971, was an occasion for celebration. Croll was in Florida for a winter holiday with some of his Toronto friends, and the group decided to mark the event by having a mock circumcision party (*bris*) on the eighth day of the baby's life. The same process was repeated after the birth of Trudeau's second son, Sacha, on 25 December 1973.

When Trudeau took over the leadership of the Liberal party, one of his principal goals was to make Canada a more congenial environment for the francophone population. The way had been paved by the *Report of the Royal Commission on Bilingualism and Biculturalism*, which strongly supported the eradication of discrimination against French Canadians outside Quebec. In the early 1970s, the passage of the Official Languages Act and a major drive to promote the use of French in the federal public service testified to a new outlook. Initially, Croll was wholeheartedly in favour of promoting the widespread use of French. He became both distressed and frustrated, however, by the administrative actions of the government on remedial measures, especially the massive program to teach French to anglophones in the federal civil service. He had originally hoped that the process would be concentrated on the introduction and improvement of French instruction in the schools. But although he had the chance on many occasions to object, he realized that if he did he might undo much of the work he had done to promote national unity through the creation of a more tolerant and caring society. And he knew just how fragile that creation was. If he even spoke out in caucus criticizing the actions of the government, the French-Canadian members would not hesitate to attack him as a bigot. Anything he might say would be subject to easy misinterpretation, and defiance of the prime minister would lessen whatever influence he had to further the lot of Canada's dispossessed. As a result, he said nothing.

Judaism was founded on righteousness, and Croll was imbued with a desire for social justice, which influenced him throughout his whole life. He felt a responsibility to do whatever he could to carry out the duties about which he had been so rigorously instructed in his formative years. In his own mind and in fact throughout his public career, he has represented Canadian Jewry and other ethnic minorities as well. With his every move followed by the press, he recognized early that if he made one false step, he would bring discredit to his family and to Jews in general. Croll has always seen himself as an exemplar or trailblazer for others.

One of the greatest tributes ever paid Croll was a reception and dinner in his honour on 30 April 1980 in Room 200 of the West Block to celebrate his eightieth birthday and the tabling of the report of the Special Senate Committee on Retirement Age Policies. Hundreds of political associates, relatives and friends attended the glittering affair. The main event of the evening was the presentation of Claude Picard's oil painting of Croll to the Speaker of the Senate, Jean Marchand, who introduced his remarks by saying:

> There are men who reflect very well their generation and know how to express themselves in a very eloquent fashion. Literature, the arts, and politics have an impressive number of these personalities who are faithful witnesses of their times.

> But the rarest and most exceptional of these witnesses are the men who have broken through the walls of their generation and opened up new pathways into the future. I believe that the Honorable Senator Croll can be counted among this group.

The leader of the Opposition in the Senate, Jacques Flynn, was equally generous, beginning his speech by describing Croll as a "wise and uncommon man; a gifted, incisive and informed politician; a warm kind and delightful personality." Croll himself spoke briefly, emphasizing again his now-familiar themes: improvement in the incomes of the elderly

poor and the scrapping of an outmoded welfare system in favour of a guaranteed annual income.

Stanley Knowles, a long-time foe of the Senate, attended
Croll's dinner and confessed to his apostasy a few weeks later
in the House of Commons:

> It is not often that I go to anything that is connected with the
> Senate. Hon. members are looking surprised—what have I
> done? A couple of weeks ago an evening testimonial dinner
> was held over in Room 200 in the West Block for Senator
> Croll on the occasion of a report in his name that had been ta-
> bled. Actually the party was supposed to have been held ear-
> lier this year, but we got into an election and the senators put
> it off. I went to that party, I admit it. I went to the party for
> the senator.
>
> I listened with a great deal of pleasure to the speeches that
> were made about Senator Croll. I listened to the very good
> humour that a number of those speakers had, but then I lis-
> tened with particular delight to David Croll's speech. He is a
> little older than I, but not much. At least he was talking about
> a portion of history in this country from the 1920s on with
> which I am very familiar. I could go along with everything he
> said in that speech, but as he got toward the end of his speech
> he said, if I quote him with reasonable correctness, that there
> are two diamonds in the crown of social legislation that we
> have built in this country and do not let anyone take away
> those two diamonds. Now, what were they? One was old age
> pensions on a universal basis and the other was medicare on a
> universal basis. Of course, one can imagine that I was ready to
> stand up and cheer when I heard Senator Croll say that. He
> elaborated on what it means to our older people to have the
> guarantee of pensions. I think it is the finest thing we have
> ever produced in this country, the concept of universality

with respect to old age security. I dislike anything that detracts from that universality. I hope we will take heed of the kind of message that Senator Croll gave that night to those who were in Room 200.[14]

On 13 March 1990, the first business of the Senate was a series of speeches celebrating David Croll's ninetieth birthday the day before.[15] There were warm tributes from all sides, and the love and respect of his colleagues was evident. The same afternoon, the Speaker of the Senate (*pro tempore*) gave a reception in his honour attended by many senators, cabinet ministers, including the prime minister, and friends from the Ottawa area, one of whom was Stanley Knowles. A most eloquent speech was made by Lowell Murray, government leader in the Senate, who broke the happy news that the prime minister had recommended to the governor general that Croll be appointed a member of Her Majesty's Privy Council for Canada. Normally this appointment is reserved for cabinet ministers, but a few others who have rendered outstanding service to the country are also admitted to the honour. The prime minister had spoken to Croll earlier about this appointment and had been most kind and gracious in his remarks. Croll had had his heart set on becoming a privy councillor for many years, so this was a birthday present that gave him great pleasure. Following the speech by Lowell Murray, Senator Allan MacEachen, leader of the Opposition in the Senate, and Herb Gray, leader of the Opposition in the House of Commons, spoke glowingly of their old friend.

Croll's actual investiture into the Privy Council took place on 21 March at Government House. This was a happy occasion, for he had known the new governor general, Ray Hnatyshyn, for many years and particularly since his election to the House of Commons in 1974. In addition, Croll and the governor general's father, Senator John Hnatyshyn, had been colleagues. Croll was treated with great deference by the officials and found the occasion very rewarding. He even drank a glass of champagne. It was a long road from the pier in Halifax where he had landed years before to exchanging pleasantries with the governor general in the luxurious surroundings of Government House.

In 1984, Croll encapsulated the liberal philosophy that had guided him so profoundly and successfully for so many years:

> Real liberalism has, as its ideology, justice with freedom, jobs, food, clothing, shelter, health and education. Those are the principles of our party and they have carried us through 50 years of office. We were the first to place welfare measures on our statute books, and the sort of liberalism that we practised yesterday, that we practise today, we shall practise tomorrow. We cannot afford to do anything less.[16]

Some three years earlier, speaking on the motion for an address to the Queen seeking the patriation of the Constitution of Canada, Croll detailed the issues that had concerned him over the years: a bill of rights, old age assistance, medicare, unemployment insurance, poverty, pensions, immigration, citizenship, a Canadian flag and the treatment of Japanese Canadians during the war. His summing up ranks with the finest speeches ever made in any parliament:

> I was privileged to be there at each small step along the way to where we stand now: I held office; I spoke in the debates; I raised my hand to vote; I helped make policy; I served on many committees, and chaired some of them; I served my constituents; I have served my party; and I have served my country. I have been in the front line in the battle for human decency in our society. So the dreams I am dreaming now are not pipe-dreams: they are founded on a clear understanding of

what can be accomplished and of what has been accomplished in this country.

I am a creature of my dreams, and they have led me to this debate, and to the great dream embodied in the resolution. I am here to remind you that the progress we have made has been won by idealism married to practical politics. And I am here to remind you as well that idealism is rooted deep in the hearts of our people, that in the end it will brook no opposition, no watering down, no endless delays, I am here to remind you that people whose memories are otherwise very short never forget when those deepest desires are frustrated.[17]

It is not given to many men to see their dreams come true.

Notes

Introduction

1. Nahum Goldmann, *The Autobiography of Nahum Goldmann: Sixty Years of Jewish Life*, trans. Helen Sebba (New York: Holt, Rinehart and Winston, 1969), 5.
2. Sholom Aleichem, *Tevye's Daughters*, trans. Frances Butwin (New York: Crown Publishers, 1949), 17.
3. Abba Eban, *My People: The Story of the Jews* (Toronto: Random House of Canada, 1968), 271.
4. See Isaiah Berlin, *Personal Impressions* (London: The Hogarth Press, 1981), 40–41.
5. Max I. Dimont, *Jews, God and History* (Toronto: Signet Books, 1969), 341.
6. Herbert Feis, *The Birth of Israel: The Tousled Diplomatic Bed* (New York: W. W. Norton and Co., 1969), 38.

Chapter 1: Setting the Stage

1. Neil F. Morrison, *Garden Gateway to Canada: One Hundred Years of Windsor and Essex County, 1854–1954* (Toronto: The Ryerson Press, 1954), 265.

2. Alan Abrams, *Why Windsor? An Anecdotal History of the Jews of Windsor and Essex County* (Windsor: Black Moss Press, 1981), 13.

3. The Croll brothers nearly lost the source of their income late in the war. Racing had been abolished in Canada for the duration, and the federal cabinet had under consideration the banning of the *Daily Racing Form* as well. *Border Cities Star*, 11 October 1918.

4. There are a number of anecdotes about the early association of Croll and Geller in Geller's autobiography. See J. D. Geller, *It's Jake with Me* (Toronto: Paperjacks, 1983).

5. *Border Cities Star*, 30 November 1918.

6. Urban Shocker also played bush-league ball for Windsor before World War I. He later pitched for the St. Louis Browns and the New York Yankees.

Chapter 2: Breaking the Barriers

1. Alan Abrams, *Why Windsor?* 21.

2. Lumby Franklin was the third mayor of Victoria, B.C., in 1886. David Oppenheimer (1834–97) was mayor of Vancouver from December 1887 until January 1892. There is a monument to him in Stanley Park. See *Detroit Jewish News*, 4 March 1955.

3. *Border Cities Star*, 2 December 1930.

4. Ibid., 4 December 1930.

5. Herbert Marshall, Frank A. Southard, Jr., Kenneth W. Taylor, *Canadian–American Industry: A Study in International Investment* (Toronto: The Ryerson Press, 1936), 63.

6. *Border Cities Star*, 6 December 1932.

7. Ibid., 12 April 1933.

8. Ibid., 30 May 1933.

9. Ibid., 1 June 1933.

10. *Toronto Daily Star*, 10 November 1933.

11. Archives of Ontario, RG 8, I-1-U (unprocessed). #206.2330.

12. *Toronto Daily Star*, 6 February 1934.

13. *Border Cities Star*, 1 June 1933.

14. "Arthur Roebuck Story" (unpublished ms.), Arthur Roebuck Papers, Public Archives of Canada, 92.
15. Neil McKenty, "Mitchell F. Hepburn and the Ontario Election of 1934," *Canadian Historical Review*, XLV, no. 4, December 1964, 301.
16. Public Archives of Canada, Mackenzie King Diaries, MG 26 J 13, 28 June 1933. The brackets and parentheses are in the typed version of the diaries in the possession of the Public Archives. It is difficult to account for the misspellings.
17. Public Archives of Canada, Oral History Project, David A. Croll, 1983.
18. Municipal Archives, Windsor Public Library, MS 6, W. F. Herman Collection, Scrapbook 7 (*Border Cities Star*, 4 June 1934).
19. Public Archives of Canada, MG 26 J 3, vol. 30, Letter, Croll to King, 22 June 1934.
20. Ontario *Gazette*, 14 July 1934.
21. Neil McKenty says in his study of Hepburn that Croll was sworn on the Talmud. Evidently McKenty was not well versed in the classic Judaic texts. *Mitch Hepburn* (Toronto: McClelland and Stewart), 60.

Chapter 3: Minister of Good Works

1. "Arthur Roebuck Story," 92.
2. *Toronto Daily Star*, 20 June 1934.
3. Archives of Ontario, RG 3, Hepburn Papers, Private, 20 March 1934.
4. David Rome, "Jewish Archival Records of 1935," *Canadian Jewish Archives* (Montreal, Canadian Jewish Congress, 1976), 100.
5. Ibid.
6. *Toronto Daily Star*, 1 January 1921.
7. Canada, House of Commons, *Debates*, 3 April 1930, 1227–28.
8. Canada, Department of Labour, *Labour Gazette*, 1937, 478. The estimates were produced by the Bank of Canada.
9. Archives of Ontario, RG 3, Box 359.

10. Croll was instructed by Hepburn to see that the coal for distribution to families on relief was bought from Alberta instead of the United States, despite the additional cost.

11. H. Blair Neatby, *William Lyon Mackenzie King, III, 1932–1939: The Prism of Unity* (Toronto: University of Toronto Press, 1976), 41.

12. Ibid., 51.

13. Joseph Schull, *Ontario since 1867* (Toronto: McClelland and Stewart, 1978), 286.

14. On this whole episode, see Christopher Anderson, *The Politics of Federalism: Ontario's Relations with the Federal Government 1867–1942* (Toronto: University of Toronto Press, 1981), 152–55.

15. Ibid., 155.

16. *Canadian Annual Review 1936 and 1937*, 196.

17. The situation deteriorated further in March 1937 when the federal grant was cut to $600,000 a month and in July to $480,000. It is curious that the doctrines of Keynes were gaining credence at just about this time.

18. *Canadian Annual Review of Public Affairs 1934*, 186.

19. Archives of Ontario, RG 3, Box 359.

20. Canada, Department of Labour, *Labour Gazette*, October 1936, 856–57.

21. Ibid., January 1937, 4.

22. Toronto *Globe*, 15 May 1935.

23. *Toronto Daily Star*, 23 May 1935.

24. Ibid., 27 July 1934.

25. *Statutes of Ontario*, 25 Geo. V, C. 19.

26. Pierre Berton, *The Dionne Years: A Thirties Melodrama* (Toronto: McClelland and Stewart, 1977), 143.

27. Municipal Archives, Windsor Public Library, MS 6, W. F. Herman Collection, Letter, Croll to Clark, 4 January 1937.

28. *Toronto Daily Star*, 25 February, 1937.

29. Municipal Archives, Windsor Public Library, MS 6, W. F. Herman Collection, Scrapbook 7, Letter, Elzire and Oliva Dionne to Croll, 29 September 1937.

30. The Rev. Garnet W. Lynd wrote to Hepburn on 23 November 1934, giving an account of Sorsoleil's speech. Archives of Ontario, RG 3, Box 320.

31. Toronto *Mail and Empire*, 22 November 1934.
32. Ibid, 23 November 1934.
33. Ibid.
34. Toronto *Mail and Empire*, 24 November 1934.
35. Archives of Ontario, RG 3, Box 230.
36. Ontario *Gazette*, 11 August 1934.
37. *Canadian Annual Review 1935 and 1936*, 237.
38. Ibid., 202.
39. The population figures are given in the draft report of the Royal Commission on Amalgamation, Municipal Archives, Windsor Public Library, Unclassified, Clerk's Department, "Amalgamation of the Border Cities 1935–36 Correspondence and Reports of the Commission of Inquiry."
40. Municipal Archives, Windsor Public Library, RG 5, HI-1/11, Town of Walkerville Council Minutes, 1934–35.
41. *Border Cities Star*, 18 April 1935.
42. Ibid.
43. In fact, Walkerville was not founded until 1890.
44. Municipal Archives, Windsor Public Library, Unclassified, Clerk's Department, "Amalgamation of the Border Cities 1935–36 Correspondence and Reports of the Commission of Inquiry."
45. Ibid.

Chapter 4: Marching with the Workers

1. Ontario *Gazette*, 25 May 1985.
2. *Canadian Annual Review 1935 and 1936*, 234.
3. *Toronto Daily Star*, 1 October 1937.
4. W. L. M. King, *Industry and Humanity* (Toronto: Thomas Allen, 1918), 72. "In some instances, women and girls had been working excessive hours, under unwholesome sanitary conditions, and had been receiving for actual work performed payments at the rate of three and four cents an hour."
5. *Globe and Mail*, 5 March 1937.
6. Ibid.
7. *Border Cities Star* (Ontario edition), 28 September 1933.
8. Murphy became governor of Michigan in 1936 and United

States attorney general in 1939 and was appointed to the Supreme Court by Roosevelt in 1940.

9. The federal attitudes are described in detail in *William Lyon Mackenzie King, III, 1932–39: The Prism of Unity*, 205. It was not until 1939 that the Supreme Court in the United States ruled that sit-down strikes were illegal.

10. Neil McKenty, *Mitch Hepburn*, 92. Although McKenty does not give the source, it may well have come from Mrs. Bruce's diary, a source of interesting tidbits of political gossip. Peter Heenan had been appointed minister of lands and forests by Hepburn in 1934.

11. *Globe and Mail*, 6 March 1937.

12. Ibid., 8 March 1937.

13. Ibid., 3 April 1937.

14. *Toronto Daily Star*, 7 April 1937.

15. Ibid., 8 April 1937.

16. A blow-by-blow account of Hepburn's dealings with the federal government is given in Neatby, *William Lyon Mackenzie King, III*, 205.

17. Roger Irwin, "The Battle for Oshawa," *The Nation*, 1 May 1937, 504.

18. Quoted in Reginald Whitaker, *The Government Party: Organizing and Financing the Liberal Party of Canada 1930–58* (Toronto and Buffalo: University of Toronto Press, 1977), 320.

19. *Toronto Daily Star*, 22 April 1937.

20. The *Toronto Daily Star* intimated on 14 April 1937 that one of its reporters, Keith Munro, was the only newspaperman involved, but there were probably others.

21. Toronto *Globe and Mail*, 15 April 1937.

22. *Toronto Daily Star*, 24 April 1937.

23. Irving Abella, ed., *On Strike: Six Key Labour Struggles in Canada 1919–1949* (Toronto: James, Lewis and Samuel, 1974), 121.

Chapter 5: Full Circle

1. *Windsor Star*, 11 August 1937.

2. Ibid., 7 October 1937.

3. Ibid.
4. Ibid.
5. *Toronto Daily Star*, 1 October 1937.
6. Ibid.
7. *Windsor Star*, 7 October 1937.
8. Ibid., 1 October 1937.
9. Ibid., 10 March 1938.
10. Ibid., 7 March 1938.
11. Alan Abrams, *Why Windsor?* 27.
12. Ibid., 71.
13. *Windsor Star*, 6 December 1938.
14. Ibid., 7 December 1938.
15. Ibid., 3 January 1939.
16. Ibid., 4 January 1939.
17. Paul Martin, *A Very Public Life, I: Far from Home*, 207.
18. *Windsor Star*, 6 June 1939.
19. Ibid., 31 August 1939.

Chapter 6: A Private War.

1. "It is sweet and honourable to die for one's country." Horace, *Odes*, 3.2.13.
2. *Windsor Star*, 2 November 1940.
3. Paul Martin, *A Very Public Life, I: Far from Home*, 355–56.

Chapter 7: The Honourable Gadfly for Spadina.

1. Labour Progressive Party or Communist Party.
2. *Globe and Mail*, 13 June 1945.
3. J. W. Pickersgill and D. F. Forster, *The Mackenzie King Record, II, 1944–45* (Toronto: University of Toronto Press, 1968), 466.
4. *Toronto Star*, 23 July 1955.
5. Canada, House of Commons, *Debates*, 3 October 1945, 722–23.
6. Ibid., 2 February 1948, 744.
7. Ibid., 5 February 1948, 899.
8. Ibid., 901.

9. Ibid.
10. 14 February 1948.
11. Canada, House of Commons, *Debates*, 4 December 1952, 335.
12. Ibid., 18 June 1947, 4386.
13. J. H. King had piloted through the House of Commons the first old age pensions bill, which received third reading on 26 May 1926 but was rejected by the Senate.
14. For a detailed account of the inner workings of the committee, see Susan Mann Trofimenkoff, *Stanley Knowles: The Man from Winnipeg North Centre* (Saskatoon: Western Producer Prairie Books, 1982), 110–12.
15. Canada, House of Commons, *Debates*, 13 April 1953, 3761–62.
16. Ibid., 3770.
17. *Globe and Mail*, 24 October 1955.
18. Special Committee on Defence Expenditures, *Minutes of Proceedings No. 1*, 7 January 1953, 25.
19. Canada, House of Commons, *Debates*, 21 April 1952, 1424.
20. Ibid., 12 January 1953, 893.
21. Special Committee, No. 5, 12 February 1953, 130.
22. Special Committee, No. 26, 5 May 1953, 815.
23. *Globe and Mail*, 13 May 1953.
24. The limited-dividend concept authorized CMHC to lend up to 90 per cent of the maximum permissible loan for a project repayable over a fifty-year period. Initially the interest on the loan was 3 3/4 per cent per annum, but the dividends paid by the sponsor could not exceed 5 per cent per annum of the ammount invested by the sponsor.
25. Canada, House of Commons, *Debates*, 9 April 1946, 693.
26. Ibid., 694.
27. Canada, House of Commons, *Debates*, 13 May 1946, 1473.
28. Ibid., 1474.
29. Canada, House of Commons, *Debates*, 24 March 1952, 715.
30. Ibid., 723.
31. Ibid., 726.
32. Ibid., 747.
33. Canada, House of Commons, *Debates*, 7 February 1955, 900.
34. Order in Council P.C. no. 946, 5 February 1943.
35. Canada, House of Commons, *Debates*, 15 March 1948, 2222.

36. *Globe and Mail*, 9 July 1947.
37. Public Archives of Canada, MG 26 J 3, vol. 30, Letter, King to Croll, 4 April 1947.
38. *Toronto Daily Star*, 22 June 1949.
39. Public Archives of Canada, MG 26 J 3, vol. 30, Letter, King to Croll, 28 June 1949.
40. Ibid., Letter, Croll to King, 8 July 1949.
41. *Toronto Daily Star*, 8 August 1953.
42. Ibid., 6 August 1953.
43. George Bain, "The Forgotten Man of Parliament Hill," *Maclean's*, 1 November 1954, 51.
44. Ibid.
45. Ibid., 52.

Chapter 8: A Friend in Need

1. Canada, House of Commons, *Debates*, 14 December 1945, 3585.
2. *Canadian Jewish Year Book 1941–1942* (Montreal: Canadian Jewish Publication Society, 1941), 221.
3. Canada, House of Commons, *Debates*, 3 April 1946, 546.
4. Ibid., 27 August 1946, 5591.
5. Ibid., 4 March 1947, 1027.
6. Ibid., 1029.
7. Ibid., 1032.
8. Order in Council P.C. no. 1734, 1 May 1947.
9. Canada, House of Commons, *Debates*, 1 May 1947, 2673.
10. Order in Council P.C. no. 2180, 6 June 1947.
11. Canada, House of Commons, *Debates*, 9 December 1949, 3036.
12. *Toronto Daily Star*, 17 June 1949.
13. Moshe Shertok changed his name to Moshe Sharett when the state of Israel was created.
14. Canada, Standing Committee of the House of Commons on External Affairs, *Minutes of Proceedings and Evidence No. 14*, 19 July 1946, 204.
15. Ibid., 206.
16. Canada, House of Commons, *Debates*, 16 July 1946, 3487.

17. Ibid., 26 February 1948.
18. Ibid., 1668.
19. Ibid., 1669.
20. Ibid., 1670.
21. *Canadian Jewish Chronicle*, 5 March 1948.
22. *Toronto Daily Star*, 17 May 1948.
23. *Ottawa Citizen*, 8 December 1948.
24. *Globe and Mail*, 25 December 1948.
25. Shimon Peres, *La Force de vaincre: Entretiens avec Joëlle Jonathan* (Paris: Editions du Centurion, 1981), 48–51.
26. *Windsor Star*, 30 October 1952.
27. *Time*, 15 December 1952, 43, and the *Toronto Daily Star*, 2 December 1952.

Chapter 9: Making the Best of It.

1. Peter Newman, *Bronfman Dynasty: The Rothschilds of the New World* (Toronto: McClelland and Stewart, 1978), 54.
2. Maxwell Henderson, "My Bronfman Years," *Saturday Night*, September 1984, 84.
3. *Windsor Star*, 29 July 1955.
4. *Globe and Mail*, 30 July 1955.
5. Ibid., 22 October 1955.
6. Canada, Senate, *Debates*, 18 January 1956, 38.
7. Ibid., 42.
8. Canada, Senate, *Debates*, 7 February 1984, 194.
9. Ibid., 14 November 1968, 542.
10. Ibid., 23 July 1963, 346.
11. Ibid., 347.
12. Canada, Senate, *Debates*, 2 February 1966, 70.
13. Ibid., 22 October 1974, 146.
14. *Final Report of the Special Committee of the Senate on Aging* (Ottawa: Queen's Printer, 1966), v.
15. A detailed study of the results of the recommendations of the committee was prepared by the Research Branch of the Library of Parliament and printed as a sixty-two-page appendix to the Senate *Debates* on 22 October 1974.

Chapter 10: The Heyday of the Consumer

1. Canada, Senate, *Debates*, 16 March 1960, 343.
2. Ibid., 11 May 1960, 561-62.
3. Ibid., 24 May 1960, 662.
4. Ibid., 14 December 1960, 164. The opinion is contained in ibid., 2 February 1961, 312-16.
5. Ibid., 23 May 1961, 695.
6. Ibid., 6 December 1962, 407.
7. Ibid., 5 June 1963, 76.
8. The establishment of the joint committee was agreed to by the Senate on 21 November 1963. Canada, Senate, *Debates*, 756.
9. *Report on Consumer Credit of the Special Joint Committee of the Senate and the House of Commons on Consumer Credit and Cost of Living* (Ottawa: Queen's Printer, 1967), 2.
10. Canada, Senate, *Debates*, 13 September 1966, 1048.
11. Canada, House of Commons, *Debates*, 8 September 1966, 8311.
12. Canada, Senate, *Debates*, 13 September 1966, 1050.
13. Ibid.
14. Canada, House of Commons, *Debates*, 9 September 1966, 8315.
15. Special Joint Committee of the Senate and the House of Commons on Consumer Credit (Prices), *Proceedings No. 28*, 17 January 1967, 2243.
16. Ibid., *Proceedings No. 27*, 20 December 1966, 2183.
17. Ibid., 16 December 1966, 2179-80.
18. *Ottawa Citizen*, 21 December 1966.
19. Special Joint Committee of the Senate and the House of Commons on Consumer Credit (Prices), *Proceedings No. 41*, 25 April 1967, 3448.
20. Canada, Senate, *Debates*, 24 May 1973, 654.
21. *Ottawa Journal*, 5 October 1978.

Chapter 11: Poverty Is No Disgrace

1. Canada, House of Commons, *Debates*, 5 April 1965, 2.
2. Economic Council of Canada, *Fifth Annual Review* (Ottawa: Queen's Printer, 1968).

3. Ibid., 136-37.
4. Canada, Senate, *Debates*, 13 September 1968, 15.
5. Ibid., 8 October 1968, 208.
6. Ibid.
7. Paul Martin, *A Very Public Life, II: So Many Worlds*, 643.
8. It was necessary to reconstitute the committee on 28 October 1969 and 9 October 1970 during the second and third sessions of the Twenty-eighth Parliament and again on 22 February 1972.
9. *Globe and Mail*, 11 November 1971.
10. In Ian Adams et al., *The Real Poverty Report* (Edmonton: M. G. Hurtig, 1971).
11. *Last Post*, Summer, 1971, vol. 1, no. 8.
12. Canada, Senate, *Debates*, 21 June 1971, 1157.
13. Canada, House of Commons, *Debates*, 17 February 1972, 3.
14. Canada, Senate, *Debates*, 14 March 1972, 129.
15. Canada, Senate, *Debates*, 29 May 1984, 606.
16. *Globe and Mail*, 18 December 1985.

Chapter 12: Retirement without Tears.

1. Canada, Senate, *Debates*, 7 December 1977, 212.
2. Canada, Senate, *Retirement without Tears* (Ottawa: Queen's Printer, 1970), 13.
3. Ibid., 132.
4. Canada, Senate, *Debates*, 31 March 1987.

Chapter 13: Family Matters and Other Adventures.

1. *Windsor Star*, 24 November 1955.
2. Ibid., 25 November 1955.
3. Ibid., 31 July 1970, and *Globe and Mail*, 31 July 1970.
4. Peter C. Newman, *The Canadian Establishment, II: The Acquisitors* (Toronto: McClelland and Stewart-Bantam, 1982), 122. Newman provides a detailed account of the Belzberg family and their financial activities.
5. Toronto *Evening Telegram*, 30 July 1965.

6. Ibid., 27 August 1965.
7. Ibid.
8. Toronto *Evening Telegram*, 28 July 1965.

Chapter 14: Winding Down

1. Donald Creighton, *Canada's First Century 1867–1967* (Toronto: Macmillan of Canada, 1970), 354.
2. Canada, Senate, *Debates*, 8 October 1968, 210.
3. Ibid., 28 January 1969, 915.
4. Ibid., 919.
5. Canada, Senate, *Debates*, 13 March 1973, 316.
6. Ibid.
7. Canada, Senate, *Debates*, 13 March 1973, 317.
8. Ibid., 654.
9. Ibid., Canada, Senate, *Debates*, 11 June 1985, 978.
10. Canada, Senate, *Debates*, 24 March 1981, 2134. The original speech was given on 9 April 1946.
11. Ibid., 2140.
12. Canada, Senate, *Debates*, 3 December 1981, 3165.
13. Ibid., 3166.
14. Canada, Senate, *Debates*, 26 May 1980, 1402.
15. Ibid., 1263–66.
16. Canada, Senate, *Debates*, 7 February 1984, 194.
17. Ibid., 24 March 1981, 2139–40.

Index

Index

Index